PREACHING

APOCALYPTIC
TEXTS

PREACHING

APOCALYPTIC TEXTS

LARRY PAUL JONES  JERRY L. SUMNEY

St. Louis, Missouri

Cover: Michael Foley
Interior Design: Wynn Younker
Art Director: Michael A. Domínguez
Cover Artwork by Gustave Doré from *Doré Gallery: Containing Two Hundred and Fifty Beautiful Engravings* by Edmund Ollier, published by Cassell, Petter, Galpin & Co.

This book is printed on acid-free, recycled paper.

Visit Chalice Press on the World Wide Web at
www.chalicepress.com

10 9 8 7 6 5 4 3 2 1   99 00 01 02 03

Library of Congress Cataloging-in-Publication Data

Jones, Larry Paul, 1952–
    Preaching apocalyptic texts / by Larry Paul Jones and Jerry L. Sumney.
      p.   cm.
    Includes bibliographical references and index.
    ISBN 0-8272-2954-2
    1. Apocalyptic literature. 2. Bible–Homiletical use. I. Sumney, Jerry L.
II. Title.
BS646.J66 1999
220'.046–dc21   99-38562
                                                        CIP

Printed in the United States of America

CONTENTS

This book comes from a class on preaching the apocalyptic texts of the Bible that the two of us have taught jointly at Lexington Theological Seminary. It reflects our commitment to understanding this important part of the canon and the central place that the worldview of apocalyptic has occupied in Christian history. We believe this material contains a theology that is necessary for the Christian community to own not only as a part of its history, but also as an important way to understand our faith in the present time. Reclaiming this part of scripture is especially important at this moment in history because too many interpreters are using it to make claims about the immediate future, particularly events around the year 2000, which this literature does not support. We, then, see this book as a call to faithful proclamation of the gospel as it has been understood from the days of the earliest church.

We thank the faculty and administration of Lexington Theological Seminary for granting us the privilege of working, thinking, and teaching together in a class that would frighten some seminaries. We also thank our students for their wrestling with this material and helping us gain insight and clarity in our interpretation and explication of apocalyptic thought and texts.

Each of the authors of this book is responsible for separate portions of the text. Larry Paul Jones authored the chapter on preaching apocalyptic and all the sermons found herein. Jerry Sumney wrote the introduction to apocalyptic and the exegesis given for each text. While composed by Larry Paul Jones, the introductory chapter, more than any other part of the book, contains the joint reflections and thoughts of the two of us. It sets out why and how apocalyptic can and must be part of the Christian community's self-understanding. The two authors of this book do not always agree about everything found here. We may disagree about some exegetical points and even about the nature of the preaching event and what should be preached from a particular text. What we agree on, however, is much larger. We agree on the basic way apocalyptic should be interpreted and that apocalyptic is an important part of the Christian tradition which needs to be included in our Christian faith.

It is with the prayer that apocalyptic will cease to be frightening to the faithful (including pastors) and will begin to give hope to its present-day readers that we offer this work to the church.

Larry Paul Jones
Jerry L. Sumney

CHAPTER 1

The Problem of Preaching Apocalyptic Texts

The Imperative of Preaching Apocalyptic Texts

Many good and faithful preachers rank preaching on apocalyptic texts alongside handling serpents; they have heard that people do it, but they have no desire to come anywhere near them. Keeping a safe distance requires little effort. Relatively few apocalyptic texts found their way into the Revised Common Lectionary, and many congregations that hear only one passage of scripture each Sunday go years without encountering an apocalyptic reading. Some may consider that too often. A professor who offered a course on "Preaching Values in the Book of Revelation" made his colleagues in the Bible faculty so uneasy that the dean came to speak with him about it![1] Apocalyptic texts make a lot of people nervous!

Yet, apocalyptic thought and texts appear throughout scripture. Each testament includes an apocalypse and apocalyptic thought lies behind or appears in many other books of the Christian Bible. The prominence and influence of apocalyptic thought even led one highly respected pastor and theologian to declare, "Apocalyptic was the mother of all Christian theology."[2]

Much of the disdain expressed over apocalyptic texts results from their misuse and abuse. Some preachers avoid Daniel, Revelation, Mark 13, and other such texts not only because they experience difficulty in interpreting them but also because they prefer not to counter or correct what others have said about them. Hence the silence in many churches when it comes

1

to apocalyptic thought. Even if we do not deem apocalyptic "the mother of all Christian theology," we dare not consider such silence golden. When we choose to remain silent on such texts, we give full interpretative authority and freedom to those who will speak. When the governor of the state of California (and future President of the United States) uses Ezekiel 38–39 to declare that when Libya "goes communist" the day of Armageddon must be near,[3] failure to counter that interpretation tacitly gives credence to it. That applies as well when radio preachers identify the beast in Revelation 13:18, whose code name is 666, as Henry Kissinger, Mikhail Gorbachev, or Bill Gates. Silence will not suffice! Whether we like it or not (and we two authors happen to like it), scripture contains ample apocalyptic material, and the people in our churches need and deserve help in understanding it and discovering the gospel messages revealed in it.

The Challenge of Preaching Apocalyptic Texts

The imperative of preaching apocalyptic texts makes the task no less daunting. This material pushes several homiletic concerns to the forefront and challenges preachers to take a stand on them. First, apocalyptic material challenges preachers to ponder with what authority they speak. The narrator in apocalyptic texts typically reports a direct revelation from God. Within the text itself, that means that the words reported by the narrator, the words of the text, have the authority of God. Whether or not their answers appear explicitly in their sermons, preachers that deal with such literature must take some stand on questions of revelation and authority. How does God reveal God's self? How can we discern which of the competing reports and experiences come from God? What is the authority of the proclaimed word and of those of us who dare to proclaim it?

Second, apocalyptic material challenges preachers to reflect on how God relates with humanity. Apocalyptic texts take the spiritual world very seriously and frequently assume the existence of spiritual beings and personified good and evil. Some of them claim that God controls human events from heaven. Preachers may define the spiritual world and the ways of God differently, but when we attempt to deal with these texts faithfully that will entail coming to terms with our own understanding of how God interacts with creation. Theological integrity and honesty further demand that preachers establish continuity between what they believe and what they preach.

Third, apocalyptic literature challenges preachers to declare who or what lays the greatest claim to their lives, to whom or what they feel most accountable. In apocalyptic texts, the narrator typically expresses profound and absolute accountability for the message received. The subsequent recipients of this message also become accountable for responding faithfully to it. For example, the prophet in the book of Revelation receives explicit instructions: "Write in a book what you see and send it to the seven churches" (Rev. 1:11). These instructions come from one wearing a long robe with a sash across his chest, whose eyes were like a flame of fire, whose feet were like burnished bronze, whose voice was like the sound of many waters, and from whose mouth came a sharp, two-edged sword (Rev. 1:13–16). After receiving this communication, the prophet falls to his feet as though dead, obviously not considering this an offer he could refuse! He then repeatedly warns the churches in the narrative (and the hearers and readers of that narrative) to listen to what the Spirit is saying to the churches (Rev. 2:7, 11, 17, 29; 3:6, 13, 22). Given the context, they (we) should not consider this an offer they (we) can refuse either! Do we? Do we consider ourselves that accountable for messages and instructions we receive from God? What imperatives motivate, drive, and define us? In the foreword to *Comfort and Protest*, Edward Huenemann describes how Allan Boesak, in solitary confinement in Pretoria, South Africa, found himself living Dietrich Bonhoeffer's conviction "not only that there are some things for which one *ought* to die but that there are some things for which one *must* die."[4] Apocalyptic thought and texts compel us to ask ourselves whether we have such a conviction. Apocalyptic thought insists that God lays an ultimate claim on our lives and calls for a radical faith based on it. To wrestle meaning from an apocalyptic text, we must decide whether or not we agree.

Fourth, apocalyptic literature challenges preachers to contemplate the relationship between the Bible and preaching. Most apocalyptic texts appear to respond to crisis situations, and they all employ powerful and seemingly esoteric images, symbols, and metaphors. How much of the historical situation must preachers identify and understand in order to have integrity while preaching a sermon based on such a text? Where can and should the "facts" about the images and metaphors used recede into the background (if they were ever uncovered at all), while preachers employ them to point toward a reality in our world? For example, can a preacher use the symbol of the tree at the center of the earth in Daniel 7 without making reference to the ancient Near Eastern mythology in which this image often appears? Similarly, can a preacher repeat the warning of Mark's Jesus to "keep awake" (Mk. 13:37) without attempting to reveal what that command probably meant to the community that first received it? All preachers may not agree on the answers to such questions—indeed, the coauthors of this book do not always agree—but that makes the questions no less important to answer. Hearers will notice if we change our hermeneutical or homiletical methods in dealing with apocalyptic texts. As responsible leaders of the church, preachers must stand willing to explain both how they employ biblical texts and why.

These concerns are not peculiar to apocalyptic texts, but the peculiar nature of apocalyptic texts makes it critical for preachers to deal with them. That alone makes it worthwhile to preach sermons based on these texts regularly. Whether or not we intend it, all of our sermons convey something about our understanding of the authority of preaching, of the ways God deals with humanity, of the nature of the claim that God lays upon us, and of the relationship between scripture and preaching. We find ourselves misunderstood on these matters often enough. Fidelity to and integrity in our task demands that we make an intentional effort to understand what the faithful and those striving to be faithful have misunderstood.

An Approach to Preaching Apocalyptic Texts

Contemporary approaches to apocalyptic texts typically follow one of two paths. Hal Lindsey, author of *The Late Great*

Planet Earth and a variety of other works, represents the first and most troublesome of these. Lindsey rummages through apocalyptic texts looking for prophecies of specific events that have happened or will happen in the contemporary world. For example, as he reads the account of the opening of the second seal in Revelation 6:4, he finds predictions of an attack on Israel by Egyptian-led Arab armies, an invasion of the Middle East by the Soviet Union [*sic*] and its allies, and the declaration of war on Russia by the People's Republic of China, all of which prepare the way for global warfare and catastrophe.[5] One wonders whether the seer had any time to reflect on his own world if his vision had so much to say about ours! As indicated earlier, political leaders also employ apocalyptic texts in this fashion. In 1971, Governor Ronald Reagan informed James Mills, President Pro Tem of the California Senate:

> In the thirty-eighth chapter of Ezekiel it says God will take the children of Israel from among the heathen, where they'd been scattered, and will gather them again in the promised land. That has finally come about after two thousand years. For the first time ever, everything is in place for the battle of Armageddon and the second coming of Christ…It can't be much longer now. Ezekiel says fire and brimstone will be rained upon the enemies of God's people. That must mean that they'll be destroyed by nuclear weapons.[6]

It seems that Ezekiel would have made a better secretary of state in the 1970s than in the sixth century B.C.E.

Whether or not we agree with the politics of such interpreters and interpretations, we must take issue with their theology and hermeneutics. First, such literalistic approaches stand on poor exegesis that ignores (and frequently violates) the historical context of the text. These texts meant something to their intended audience. They can and do speak to us, but they were not written for or about us. Second, these approaches reflect and convey a deterministic view of history that leaves little or no room for responsible Christian action in and for a troubled world. Christians need only to become (self-)righteous Jonahs sitting in the shade waiting for the calamity to begin. Third, these approaches scorch the hope of the gospel with the menacing flames of their "apocalyptic terrorism."[7] They promote a fear of the Lord that leads to neither wisdom nor fidelity but to debilitating trepidation.

The second approach to apocalyptic literature characteristic of our times seeks to individualize the messages of apocalyptic texts. The images and metaphors of the text become vehicles to aid individuals on their personal quest for meaning, and the apocalyptic narrative becomes a personalized account of an individual's journey toward God. Augustine planted the seeds of this approach when he interpreted apocalyptic texts as allegories of the moral struggles of the soul. Those seeds sprouted vigorously at the end of the nineteenth century, when Johannes Weiss sought to reinterpret the apocalyptic portions of the message of Jesus as a reference to the end all of us eventually face, death.[8] While these approaches may take the context of the reading more seriously, avoid the determinism of more literalistic interpretations, and express the hope of the gospel, their focus on the individual stands in stark contrast to an essential feature of apocalyptic thought. The faith that stands behind and finds expression in apocalyptic texts "is not an individualistic phenomenon but one that always appears in the context of a cohesive and relatively well organized group."[9] Stated crudely, apocalyptic texts are about God and community; they are not about "me and you, God." The letters to the seven churches that open the book of Revelation speak first and foremost to communities. The vision of Daniel 7 appeals not to isolated individuals but to "the people of the holy ones of the Most High" (Dan. 7:27; cf. 7:18, 25). Apocalyptic thought holds individuals accountable and offers words of hope to them, but first and foremost it emerges from, addresses, and seeks the benefit of the community. Apocalyptic thought will not allow individuals to escape into themselves to find meaning in an often troubling world. It challenges the community of faith to be the gathered and identifiable people of God in that world.

How, then, should we approach apocalyptic literature? First, it seems imperative to remember that apocalyptic texts came from distinct historical settings and that they addressed communities that found themselves "out of sync" with the surrounding culture, society, and world. In those crisis situations, the authors of these materials called people of faith to recognize that they owed their primary, if not exclusive, allegiance to God. Daniel sought to offer a word of hope to Jews suffering persecution at the hands of Antiochus IV Epiphanes. Although we cannot date it as precisely, Revelation addressed Christians experiencing hostility because of their identity and what they believed. Historical dates and situations need not dominate or even appear in every sermon on an apocalyptic text, but to understand apocalyptic literature we must take those historical contexts into consideration. Second, as we attempt to hear in these texts a timely word from God, we must keep our focus on the community. Although contemporary Christians in the United States may not face systematic persecution, apocalyptic texts challenge us to name those places where we are out of sync with the world around us because of what we believe and because of our allegiance to the God who lays claim to us. Walter Brueggemann aids in this endeavor in his description of the church as a community of exiles,[10] as do Stanley Hauerwas and Will Willimon as they characterize believers as resident aliens living in the Christian colony.[11] Persecuted or not, as a group of people that lives in the world while defining itself as distinct in (thus, apart from) the world, we can approach apocalyptic texts asking where the gospel calls us to answer to an authority beyond and greater than the world and where our conviction that God will "win in the end" demands specific acts and attitudes of faith here and now.

CHAPTER 2

Apocalyptic Thought

How do you experience the world? Is it fair or unfair? Good or evil? Redeemable or beyond hope? You probably do not want to choose either alternative in the questions just asked. Most people today find the truth somewhere in between these extremes. If that is the case for you, then apocalyptic writings will be somewhat foreign to your way of thinking. Though we do not often think about it, our individual theology has been influenced by our experience of the world. What we think about God, the world, and other humans (just to name a few things) is significantly affected by what has happened to us and how we interpret those events. If we are going to understand apocalyptic writings, we will need to know something about the ways the authors of such works think so that we can begin to understand why they speak as they do about God, God's people, and God's enemies.

Apocalyptic writers usually view the world as completely captured by evil and as irredeemable without a catastrophic intervention of God. In their experience, there is something drastically wrong with the world. Apocalyptic writers are seeking a way to reconcile their belief in a good, powerful, and just God and their encounter with pervasive and successful evil.

In theological terms, one of the most basic issues apocalyptic thought wrestles with is theodicy: How does one explain injustice and evil in the world while holding to belief in a good and just God? This question is asked explicitly in several apocalyptic writings. In 2 Esdras,[1] the leading character looks about himself and sees the great sinfulness of the Babylonians who

9

have conquered Israel. His question is, "Are the deeds of those who inhabit Babylon any better [than those of Israel]?" (2 Esd. 3:28). Then he complains that no one can understand what God has done and that God has given no explanation (see 3:28–4:36).

Apocalyptic arises in situations where the questions of theodicy become acute. The problem of evil in the world is always with us, but it becomes more important for an individual or a group when it is brought home, when you are the good person who is suffering unjustly. Groups adopt an apocalyptic outlook in times of crisis, when it seems they are being overwhelmed by their enemies, enemies who are beyond their capacity to defeat. Apocalyptic helps such groups interpret their experience in a way that preserves and strengthens their faith in God. Examples of such groups from the ancient world include the inhabitants of Qumran (who wrote the Dead Sea Scrolls), Jews living at the time of the Maccabean revolt (see the discussion of the setting of Daniel in chapter 4), and Christians facing persecution. All of these groups faced overwhelming opposition or defeat, while believing they were God's people. All asked, "How can God allow this? How will God respond to this?" Apocalyptic thought addresses these questions.

Apocalyptic responds by pointing beyond history, by asserting that the ultimate answer to these questions lies in another realm. So it gives a larger context in which to understand the events of the world. It argues that earthly events are only one part of a cosmic drama that involves forces most people are unaware of but that are now being revealed to God's people. It asserts that God will set things right in the end, that God's justice will be exercised. This satisfaction of God's justice includes both punishing the wicked and rewarding the group's faithfulness. On a personal level, apocalytpic says that the last word is not said when you die, for there are rewards for the faithful individual.

Some Common Characteristics of Apocalyptic Writings

To understand the apocalyptic material in the Bible it is useful to look at some common characteristics of apocalyptic writings. By recognizing these characteristics, we will find apocalyptic texts more accessible and more profitable sources for Christian thought about, and response to, the world we know.

Apocalyptic writings are usually pseudepigraphic, that is, written by someone other than the person by whom the document claims to be written.[2] While this sounds like plagiarism to us, it was a widespread practice in the ancient world. Works were written in the name of Socrates more than three hundred years after he died. Writers often used this technique when they thought they represented the thought of the claimed writer and so could bring the earlier person's insight to bear on the actual writer's situation. Jewish and Christian apocalyptic writings often claim to be written by someone known from the Bible who lived long before the actual writing (e.g., Enoch, Ezra, Baruch, Abraham, etc.).

Apocalyptic writings claim that they contain a revelation from God, which consists of knowledge that has been hidden from all but a very few people but is now revealed to the wider circle of the people of God because the end is near. They often contain information about angels, the ordering of the cosmos, or the nature of heavenly realms. This knowledge is usually given to the writer by an angelic mediator. The writer's claim to authority comes primarily from the assertion that what is written is a revelation directly from God.

Connected with their pseudonymity, apocalyptic writings often include *ex eventu* prophecy. This means that their supposed writer predicts something that is future for that figure but is a past event for the real author. When Enoch, who is taken from Genesis 5, has correctly predicted the history of the world from the flood to the second century B.C.E. (when it was actually written), the reader has good reason to think he will also be right about what is to come next. So *ex eventu* prophecy gives assurance to the reader that what the writer says is trustworthy. This sure word is precisely what those who are suffering need.

Finally, the most basic point apocalyptic writers want to establish is that God will make things right. All apocalyptic thought asserts that God will be true to God's own nature by defeating evil and establishing justice for the faithful. God will establish a reign of justice and goodness that evil cannot overcome. The readers can take courage, even in the most dire circumstances, that this is the certain end and that they will be included in this victory of God. All the other characteristics of apocalyptic are intended to help establish this point.

Not all apocalyptic texts have all of these characteristics (for example, Revelation has no *ex eventu* prophecy), but they give us a place to start as we investigate this material.

The Origins of Apocalyptic Thought

Our understanding of apocalyptic thought will also be enhanced if we know something about the origins of this type of thought. Two related questions bear on this issue: When did apocalyptic thought emerge? and What are its sources? We begin with the second question. There have been many suggestions about where the roots of apocalyptic thought are to be found. Some have argued that it drew only on Hebrew prophetic thought, others that it was derived solely from Wisdom traditions, and still others that the strongest influences came from Persian or Greek thought. Most interpreters think apocalyptic thought drew on all of these resources when facing certain types of social circumstances.

Most interpreters also agree that the primary source for apocalyptic is Hebrew prophecy. The faith of the Hebrew prophets always had an eschatological orientation. They believed in a God who worked in the world and who would bring about God's own purposes, including establishing the triumphant rule of God. The prophets never doubted that God's purposes would win out in the end. Apocalyptic thought refocuses this belief, giving more emphasis to the final conclusion. Given that the return from exile did not begin a period of national prominence in which God was clearly ruler of the world and given the failure of other nationalistic hopes expressed by the prophets, apocalyptic thought relocated those hopes outside the realm of history. They began to look for their fulfillment in a more dramatic movement by God, an action that affected history but was brought in from another realm.

In addition to this stream of thought from the prophets, apocalyptic drew in characteristics often found in the Wisdom tradition. Daniel is an interpreter of dreams, a function usually associated with wise men rather than prophets. Daniel, the leading character in the apocalyptic book that bears his name, is even ranked among the "wise men" in Babylonia (Dan. 4:6–8). Additionally, some of the determinism found in Wisdom thought was appropriated as apocalyptic thought developed. Apocalypticists are certain about the outcome of history and the main lines of the course of history. This is seen not only in their confidence that God's reign will be established, but also in the foretelling of world history found in many apocalyptic texts. This certainty about the course of history and its ultimate outcome does not necessarily mean that human free will is diminished. In apocalyptic thought, humans are free to make their own choices about whether they will be on God's side or that of evil. So some events of history are determined, but it is up to the individual to respond to God appropriately. The importance of free will can also be seen in the apocalyptic writers' belief that individuals will be judged by God.

The prophetic and Wisdom traditions cannot, however, account for all one finds in apocalyptic. It seems clear that its dualism, its development of traditions about angels, and its cosmology are significantly influenced by Greek and Persian thought. So, many sources contributed to the kind of thought that is found in apocalyptic writings. Materials from these various traditions were combined and synthesized to create a way of thinking, a way of perceiving God, the world, and themselves that made sense of the addressed communities' experience.

What finally brings all these influences together into what we recognize as apocalyptic thought are the circumstances of life faced by particular communities. While no one type of situation can be said to produce apocalyptic, it may be broadly characterized as crisis literature. It developed when communities were under great stress, stress that threatened their belief in the power, goodness, and justice of God. Sometimes this was a national crisis, other times it was simply a crisis for the group. So the best terms to describe the situations in which apocalyptic thought did (and does) develop are relative deprivation and cognitive dissonance. In a situation that involves relative deprivation, the group is deprived of some status, position, authority, or other value they believe they should have but do not, in fact, possess. So a comparatively well-off group could develop an apocalyptic mind-set if they were convinced they were being deprived of something of significant value because of their religious beliefs. This experience of opposition from those outside the group can arise from circumstances that are not historically significant but nevertheless have a great impact on the group affected. It is the experience of oppression that is important for the development of apocalyptic thought, not the historical significance of what causes the group to feel this way.

The term *cognitive dissonance* may also be appropriately applied to many such situations. This expression describes a situation in which there is significant disparity between what one thinks and what one experiences. Again, this does not have to be a circumstance that has a noticeable effect on world or even local history; it simply involves a perceived great difference between what one expects and thinks ought to be and what is felt to be the reality. In our cases, those who believe they are God's people expect this identity to enhance their status, but just the opposite seems to be happening. For early Christians, becoming part of the Christian movement meant they had begun to worship the only true God. They gave up participation in other cults to be associated with this God. But instead of leading to blessings and good fortune, it led to disadvantage and persecution. Such experiences could be interpreted as evidence that they had made the wrong choice. Apocalyptic thought tries to reconcile who the people of God know themselves to be and what they think that identity means with the ways they perceive their existence at that moment in time.

Whether seen more as cognitive dissonance or relative deprivation, apocalyptic develops in situations in which a group feels deprived and sees the world to be in a crisis. Things are not what they should be or, more important, what God wants them to be. Since the group is powerless to change the situation, the only solution is an act of God, an act in which God destroys the current world order and establishes an order in which justice and goodness are dominant.

The type of situation described here as that which provides fertile ground for the seeds of apocalyptic to grow was present in the second century B.C.E. in Palestine. As the discussion of the historical context of Daniel in chapter 4 will show, this was a period in which people were persecuted and killed precisely because they were remaining faithful to God. This seems to be the moment when the various elements of the mix came together to form what we know as apocalyptic. It is at this point that belief in judgment after death and in the resurrection of the righteous take hold within Judaism. By this moment in history the Jews have had extensive exposure to Persian and Greek ideas and they have had to begin to reinterpret the messages of the prophets because their hopes for national prominence have not materialized. Thus, apocalyptic thought comes to prominence in the desperate struggle in Judea, probably between 200 and 150 B.C.E.

Some Important Aspects of Apocalyptic Thought

It will also help us understand apocalyptic texts if we know something about how most apocalyptic writers think about God, the nature of humanity, and ethics.

The Nature of God in Apocalyptic Thought

The topic of the nature of God is not a common one in apocalyptic writings, but some characteristics of God stand out as very important for this way of thinking. This topic is also important because maintaining belief in God is one of the primary functions of apocalyptic thought. As a means to help us understand apocalyptic, we will focus our attention on three matters: God's transcendence, sovereignty, and justice.

All apocalyptic writers agree that God is personal, powerful, and holy, but there is a debate among scholars over whether apocalyptic thought reflects a view of God that sees God as increasingly transcendent and so less immanent. Some scholars see the rise of a developed angelology as a sign that God is no longer as accessible as God had been when the prophets spoke of God as a parent. In some apocalyptic writings, angels seem to be the link between God and the world; occasionally angels even appear as mediators between God and people who pray.

However, in some of these same writings (e.g., 1 Enoch[3]) we find other acts of God performed immediately with no mediation. Additionally, in books such as Daniel the characters obviously have direct access to God in prayer and God acts directly throughout the stories. Other apocalyptic writings teach that God acts directly among humans (e.g., 2 Esd.). What we find, then, is that apocalyptic works do not all agree on this matter, but those who think God is accessible only through intermediaries are a distinct minority. Furthermore, a developed angelology does not necessarily mean that God is thought to be distant. The War Scroll from Qumran has an extensively developed angelology, but it also has God "in our midst" in the final battle. What all of these apocalyptic writers do agree on is that God must be separated from the evil in the world. All of them see God's holiness as inviolable. Thus, while God may be in direct contact with the world, God does not come into contact with evil.

Belief in the sovereignty of God is essential for apocalyptic. One main point of apocalyptic writings is to assure the readers that, in spite of evidence to the contrary, God is sovereign. We see this in the confidence these writers have that the plan of God is moving forward. It is further demonstrated in the extensive *ex eventu* prophecy found in some apocalyptic writings. These elements of apocalyptic discourse, elements that are evidence for a historical determinism, show that these writers believe that history, at least its main outline and final outcome, has been ordained and arranged by God. The certainty of God's final victory is central to apocalyptic thought. This theme stands out especially clearly in Daniel. In the story in which Nebuchadnezzar becomes like an animal, Daniel declares to the king three times (4:17, 25, 26) that God is sovereign, and the story ends with Nebuchadnezzar's acknowledging this very point (4:34). God's sovereignty is also a theme that runs through all the visions of Daniel 7–12.

This point is important in apocalyptic writings because the writers and the readers seem to be living in a world that is ruled by evil, a world in which God is not sovereign. In fact, most apocalyptic thinkers are convinced that the world is not currently ruled by God. This is certainly the viewpoint of the New Testament writers. Though most Christians today are used to thinking that God is in control of our lives and our world, apocalypticists were (and are) convinced that this was not the case. They emphasize that the current domination of the world by evil is temporary. They assert that even though the world is presently ruled by the forces of evil, the true sovereign of the entire cosmos will soon act. The God who is the ultimate King will reclaim what rightfully belongs to God and will punish the usurpers along with their accomplices and will reward those who have been faithful to God. Without such a belief in the sovereignty of God, apocalyptic—indeed, all Christian faith—cannot exist.

Apocalypticists are also convinced that God is just. Belief in the justice of God is another primary motivation for apocalyptic thought. That the world is ruled by evil and that the righteous are those who suffer most are problems only if one believes God is just. So apocalyptic seeks ways to show that God's justice will be exercised and will be the final word. This belief is manifested in the development of the ideas of judgment after death and of the resurrection.

Judgment is a central characteristic of apocalyptic thought. At the heart of all apocalyptic speculation about judgment is the conviction that God will not let God's people be destroyed by their enemies. Judgment is necessarily related to their belief in the justice of God because, for justice to reign, evil must be punished and good must be rewarded (see 1 Enoch 102:1; 103:1–104:8). This is a logically necessary element of belief in a just (i.e., fair) God. So in the face of persecution, the ethical faiths of Judaism and Christianity opted for the belief that God's righteousness is exercised in a realm beyond earthly life. Judgment in apocalyptic is usually based on morality. In Judaism this meant faithfulness to the Law; in Christianity it meant adhering to Christian morality as understood in a particular community and not denying the faith in persecution.

It was also this belief in the justice of God that led to the belief in the resurrection of the dead within Judaism. The idea of an afterlife that offered more than fading away in Sheol had been growing within Judaism, but it was the events associated with the Maccabean revolt (see the introduction to Daniel) that finally resulted in a fairly widespread belief in the resurrection of at least some of the dead. Just before and during the time of this revolt, Jews were executed precisely for being faithful to God and the Torah (see the graphic story of the torture and execution of seven brothers and their mother in 4 Maccabees 7[4]). Such terrible events, of course, push the question of the justice of God to the forefront. How can God be just and allow people to be tortured to death for their faith? Since God did not rescue these martyrs as God rescued the faithful in the stories of Daniel, there must be some other way in which the justice of God is satisfied. God's justice demands that the righteousness and faithfulness of these martyrs be rewarded. Because of this divine necessity, belief in an afterlife for the righteous flowered in this period. At the beginning, only the extraordinarily righteous, or martyrs, and the extraordinarily wicked had an afterlife, but as time passed most Jews came to believe that all persons participated in the afterlife.[5] So belief in a resurrection that included judgment grew out of the injustices experienced by communities that held firmly to their belief in a sovereign and just God.

We should not think that judgment based on morality requires that apocalypticists be legalists. That is far from the case. Only a very few apocalyptic writings (e.g., 3 Bar.[6]) assert that judgment is based solely on one's deserts. Most acknowledge that people are found righteous in judgment only through God's grace and mercy. God's grace does not impede the exercise of God's justice: They are necessarily cooperative but equally necessary. Again, judgment based on morality does not mean judgment without grace and it does not mean legalism. The Qumran War Scroll (chapter 11) states that God delivers God's people through God's loving-kindness and not according to their works. Similarly, 2 Esdras trusts that since humans cannot overcome their evil tendency, God will supply grace at judgment. When apocalypticists think of judgment, fear is not their first thought.

Rather, this is the moment when retribution is meted out to their enemies and God's. They certainly do not lose sight of the accountability judgment brings to them, but they trust God to fulfill God's purposes and nature by bringing them into the place God has prepared for God's people.

The idea of God's being just in judgment makes modern people nervous. We are more ready to focus our attention on God's love and mercy, thinking that these are the opposite of justice. But they are not. If God is not just, then God is unjust. The alternative to God's being just is that God is unfair, that God plays favorites or is capricious. This unhappy alternative would mean we could never trust God. Furthermore, the justice of God is the basis for all Christian calls for justice in the world. Since Christian ethics is based on the character of God, we have no basis for working for justice, including equal rights for all people, unless we believe in the unshakable justice of God. So apocalyptic brings us back to a characteristic of God with which we are less than comfortable, but which is essential to who God is and to what makes God a God we can trust and a God who is worthy of worship.

Human Nature in Apocalyptic Thought

To understand the view of human nature seen in our material we must begin with a survey of how human nature was seen in the Hebrew Bible. Instead of one consistent view, one finds a development in thought within Israel about human nature. In the traditions found in the Pentateuch, the individual was not as important as the group. One's family or tribe always took precedence over the individual. This emphasis on the group meant that the way one lived on after death was through what she or he had contributed to the well-being of the group. Thus, the afterlife for individuals was envisioned only to a very limited extent. When people died they went to a place called Sheol, at least temporarily. This was not a pleasant place, but a place where one was powerless, where one could not even remember the goodness of Yahweh. There were no moral distinctions in Sheol, and eventually one faded out of existence.

The prophets began to give more importance to the individual. The emphasis was still on the group, and the reward of the righteous was primarily the good of Israel and of one's descendants, but some ideas about the continuance of the individual emerged. The importance of the individual is shown especially clearly in Jeremiah and Ezekiel. In Ezekiel 18, the result of people's sin is to be visited on them alone rather than on their children (or, by extension, their nation). This separation of the fate of the individual from that of the group is a somewhat different perspective from the one we see in the Pentateuch and is the sort of thought that prepares the way for the views we find in apocalyptic.

All apocalypticists believe that humans continue to exist after death. As we have already seen, the experiences of persecution and martyrdom seemed to require some avenue other than what happens in this world for the expression of God's righteousness and justice. Clearly martyrs were not dealt with justly in this world. Outside the thought of apocalyptic, martyrs were sometimes seen as receiving the punishment due the nation, thus paving the way for Israel's restoration. But the continuing unfaithfulness of some in Israel seemed to make national restoration impossible. So personal rewards and punishments became the ways by which God responded to faithfulness and wickedness. Beyond this concern about justice, the desire for continued fellowship with God and with the fellow faithful pushed forward the belief in an afterlife with rewards and punishments. This belief could also be seen as a type of fulfillment of national hopes, since the individual was not blessed in isolation but with others who were faithful.

With the exception of a very few documents (most notably Jubilees[7]), apocalyptic writers (including the apostle Paul) envisioned the afterlife as a resurrection of the body, not as the immortality of the soul. The idea of a resurrection of the body is consistent with the Hebrew idea that a human is a unitary psycho-physical unit. That is, the Hebrews did not separate the body and soul, giving the soul a higher value, as the Greeks had done. Thus, a person cannot be complete or happy without both body and soul. Sheol had been a place where one had no body; such existence could only be temporary and could not be considered true life. So apocalyptic continued to see human personality as a unity rather than as a duality. Believing in the resurrection of the body did not mean that life was always conceived of as bound to material, earthy existence. Rather, they sometimes looked forward to the transformation of the body, a transformation that suited the body for life with God. A fairly extended explication of this notion is found in 1 Corinthians 15.

Ethics in Apocalyptic Thought

In this section we turn our attention to what humans are held accountable for in apocalyptic thought. Only a very few scholars of apocalyptic have argued that apocalyptic has no concern for ethics because it has separated the kingdom of God from earthly realities. As this view has it, apocalyptic, rather than being socially responsible, becomes preoccupied with the damnation of the oppressor or with blessings in another realm. Though this is a common perception about apocalyptic thought among nonspecialists, most scholars reject this interpretation, and many assert that ethics is central to apocalyptic.

The expectation of judgment found in all apocalyptic implies that ethics is central even when it is not explicitly discussed. One of the primary reasons authors wrote apocalyptic texts was to encourage faithfulness to God and loyalty to the Law of God, even if it leads to death. All apocalyptic is hortatory. Discourses that encourage ethical living and that specify what that means are common in apocalyptic texts. Encouraging faithful (i.e., ethical) living was a primary goal of Daniel 1–6, and in 2 Esdras the sole characteristic of the saved is holiness. Another indicator of the importance of ethics in this way of thinking is the way life in the messianic future is described: It is in accordance with God's law.

In Jewish apocalypses, the Law was the ethical ideal both now and in the age to come. The authors of these texts saw no antagonism between being required to keep the Law and echatological confidence. In their view, both the Law and apocalyptic actions by God were expressions of God's covenant with them and thus were blessings.

Given the emphasis on judgment found in apocalyptic thought, it is not surprising that individual accountability is important. People are accountable before God for their transgressions of God's law and will. The unfaithful are accountable because they have refused the ways of God. Thus, the distinctions among those who have died are based on their conduct while on earth. This does not mean apocalypticists were legalists, for most of them recognized that the only way anyone could stand before God was if God exercised mercy.

Some interpreters argue that the apocalyptic outlook leads to a passive ethic, an ethic which encourages people simply to submit to persecution. Some apocalyptic works (for example, the Assumption of Moses)[8] do recommend quietism, but this seems to be against the general trend. The Jewish uprisings throughout the Roman period show that apocalyptic is often not passive because many of these revolts were tied to apocalyptic hopes. Most of these many rebellions, and they were numerous, expected God to intervene to overthrow the Romans and to establish those who instigated the uprising, who identified themselves as God's people, in positions of power. The War Scroll of Qumran offers us a specific example of this way of thinking. Its author expects the community to be active participants in the endtime battle. Many apocalyptic groups clearly thought they had an active role to play in God's plan.

Though some have asserted that apocalyptic's attention to the future world leads people to be unconcerned about present conditions in this world, that is not necessarily the case. The Damascus Document, which was written for laypeople associated with the Qumran community and therefore expresses an apocalyptic worldview, has a clear concern for social justice (see especially chapter 1). Second Enoch also encourages social justice through its attention to issues involving money, the courts, and the poor. So apocalyptic does not entirely abandon the world to evil. The people of God are expected to act justly and to work for a more just world, even though the forces against them are overwhelming.

Conclusion

It is hoped that this brief introduction to apocalyptic thought will prepare the reader to understand better the texts we address in this book. The writings we will look at come from a variety of genres, yet they all participate in the thought world described here. These writings are all seeking ways to make sense of their belief in a good, powerful, and just God given their experience of the world as a place ruled by evil. They do this mainly by asserting that God will act soon in ways that decisively vindicate God's nature as they understand it. At the same time, they also want to encourage their readers to remain faithful to God in very difficult circumstances.

CHAPTER 3

Characteristics of an Apocalyptic Preacher

Shortly after daybreak every Sunday morning, a local television station broadcasts a program led by a preacher who follows Barth's advice and holds a Bible in one hand and a newspaper in the other. He draws attention to a series of headlines about everything from a new type of cancer cell to reports of hurricanes and famines, and then faces the camera to declare earnestly, "Every one of the headlines you have heard was predicted in the Bible." He plucks a variety of apocalyptic verses out of their contexts and reads them as proof of his point. As the introduction stated, that is not what we have in mind when we talk about the apocalyptic preacher.

Apocalyptic preachers know the hazards of attempting to interpret apocalyptic and all other biblical texts. They know that the often bizarre images of apocalyptic literature and the abuse of such texts by individuals who equate prophecy with predicting the future have frightened away many of the faithful. But they still insist that apocalyptic texts deserve to be heard. They consider the contribution of apocalyptic thought essential to Christian theology and they endeavor to allow apocalyptic texts to influence both the content and the intent of their sermons. The following discussion of characteristics of the apocalyptic preacher will attempt to describe that influence. Many of the characteristics discussed apply to all preachers. No preacher or sermon at any particular point in time will exhibit all of these characteristics. But, individually and collectively, these traits become evident when preachers allow

apocalyptic texts and thought to contribute to their understanding of the gospel and to their preaching ministry.

*The apocalyptic preacher strives to make the members of the com-
munity of faith feel oppressed by prevailing norms, culture, and power
structures.* In Mark 13, often called the "Synoptic Apocalypse,"
Jesus anticipates the destruction of the temple and then warns
believers: "As for yourselves, beware; for they will hand you
over to councils; and you will be beaten in synagogues; and
you will stand before governors and kings because of me, as a
testimony to them...and you will be hated by all because of
my name" (Mk. 13:9, 13a). The text addresses not simply a
gathering of pessimists or isolated individuals suffering from
paranoia, but a community of believers experiencing hardships
because of their faith. Recently, scholars have raised questions
about the long-held assumption that a crisis stands behind every apocalyptic text.[1] Even, however, if no specific crisis pro-
duced apocalyptic thought in general or each apocalyptic text
in particular, apocalyptic literature seeks to create a sense of
crisis among its readers. The apocalyptic preacher knows that
being a people of faith means daring to be identifiably different from others in the society. The apocalyptic preacher further knows that daring to be identifiably different results at
least in opposition and often in persecution and oppression.
This feeling of oppression, of being held back and kept unful-
filled, draws the group together for mutual support and conso-
lation and also motivates the members to accept the radical
claim laid upon them by the God of apocalyptic thought.

Please remember that the apocalyptic preacher insists that
no claim on our lives has greater legitimacy or authority than
that of God. Influences and demands that stand in the way of
that claim are not simply different, they are harmful and wrong.
For example, as many contemporary church leaders look de-
spairingly at declining membership roles, they opt to follow
the lead of successful advertisers and learn from them what it
takes to fill the pews. In our consumer-oriented society, they
want the church to exercise greater savvy in protecting and
expanding its market share, to do a more effective job of at-
tracting and feeding consumers of ecclesiological goods. An

apocalyptic preacher, on the other hand, would identify the rampant consumerism in our society as an influence that threatens the faithful. Slick advertisements that create a hunger for more and more oppose the message of the gospel and erode the quality of life in the faith community. The apocalyptic preacher will insist that the presence and power of that influence creates a crisis for the church to which the faithful must respond. That does not mean that the apocalyptic preacher demands that the faithful either take up arms in militant resistance or withdraw from society; but the apocalyptic preacher will insist that the community of faith identify this threat and take measures to protect itself from it. Yes, this sounds sectarian! Can and should a group that defines itself as "in the world but not of the world" remain true to itself and avoid all charges of sectarianism? The apocalyptic preacher states without equivocation that the surrounding culture not only is *not* Christian but also is *against* Christianity. Allowing cultural norms to shape or to prevail in the community of faith would mean ignoring the gospel and losing the identity of the church. The apocalyptic preacher wants the church to have absolute certainty about whose it is and what it is, and, in order to meet this end, does not shirk from labeling the prevailing culture as dangerous, oppressive, and sinful.

The community of faith could interpret this danger and oppression as a sign of God's disfavor. While apocalyptic thought makes ample room for the judgment of God, the troubles that beset the community of faith do not result from that. Rather, in the midst of its distress the community remains beloved by God. *The apocalyptic preacher works to convince the hearers that God notices and cares for the community of faith and for the individual.* Even when evil runs rampant in the surrounding society and the influences of that society bear down on the faith community, God keeps a watchful and caring eye on them. The "Isaiah Apocalypse" (Isa. 24:1–27:13), for example, certainly renders words of God's judgment on the earth. The opening verses announce:

> Now the LORD is about to lay waste the earth and
>   make it desolate,

and he will twist its surface and scatter its
   inhabitants.
And it shall be, as with the people, so with the priest;
      as with the slave, so with his master;
      as with the maid, so with her mistress;
   as with the buyer, so with the seller;
      as with the lender, so with the borrower;
      as with the creditor, so with the debtor.
The earth shall be utterly laid waste and utterly
   despoiled;
for the LORD has spoken this word. (Isa. 24:1–3)

All the unfaithful will feel the weight of God's judgment,
but words of tenderness and compassion describe God's dealings with the faithful:

For you have been a refuge to the poor,
      a refuge to the needy in their distress,
      a shelter from the rainstorm and a shade from the
      heat.
When the blast of the ruthless was like a winter
   rainstorm,
      the noise of aliens like heat in a dry place,
   you subdued the heat with the shade of clouds;
      the song of the ruthless was stilled. (Isa. 25:4–5)

Without doubt, the community lives in hard times, but they
are not bereft of the presence and care of God.

We often find ourselves lulled or led into the belief that
when we experience adversity we must have done something
to offend God, and when we experience good fortune or
prosperity we must have done something to please God. The
apocalyptic preacher recognizes the fallacy of such thought.
Obedience to God often results in struggle and suffering. As
previously noted, being a people of faith means daring to be
identifiably different from others, and daring to be identifiably
different results at least in opposition, if not in persecution and
oppression. In Daniel 3, for example, Shadrach, Meshach, and
Abednego found themselves in the flames of adversity not because they had offended God but because they had attempted
to remain faithful to God. Indeed, the story wants to convince

the faithful that God remained with them and continued to care for them despite the plots of those who stood against them.

The apocalyptic preacher does not make light of the tribulations of the faithful, but will not allow the faithful to blame God for them. God cares for the faith community even when no one else does. The apocalyptic preacher repeats this assurance often and with conviction. In the midst of the description of events surrounding the destruction of the temple, Matthew's Jesus informs the disciples, "If those days had not been cut short, no one would be saved; but for the sake of the elect those days will be cut short" (Mt. 24:22). Even amid times of unparalleled wickedness, God keeps a watchful and concerned eye on the faithful. When Paul speaks of times of darkness and inescapable destruction, he also reminds his readers, "God has destined us not for wrath but for obtaining salvation through our Lord Jesus Christ, who died for us, so that whether we are awake or asleep we may live with him" (1 Thess. 5:9–10). Yes, opposition and even oppression will come, but God's interest in and concern for the faithful remain steadfast.

This assurance of the presence and care of God flows from the conviction that there is more to life than meets the eye. *The apocalyptic preacher believes and attempts to help others to believe that "this is not all there is," that there is power, goodness, and justice beyond and above that seen and experienced in the world.* This belief reflects not a naive and romanticized notion that everything will work out for the best in the end, but an unshakable certainty that nothing can rival the ultimate sovereignty of God, whose plans and intentions transcend the limits of human experience and even human imagination.

A clear biblical expression of this occurs in Revelation 8–11 in the narration of the blowing of the seven trumpets and the events associated with those blasts. When the first six angels blow their trumpets, hail, fire, and blood come crashing into the earth, one third of the creatures of the sea perish, a great star falls from heaven and the radiance of the sun and the heavenly lights diminish by one third, the land endures a plague of locusts, and one third of humanity dies. Despite all of this, humanity remains unrepentant. Such a turn of events leaves little, if any, room for optimism. The world seems bereft of

hope. God appears to have gambled with creation and lost.
Then comes the sounding of the seventh trumpet. Instead of
seeing everything brought to an end, we hear those worshiping God in heaven sing:

> We give you thanks, Lord God Almighty,
>   who are and who were,
> for you have taken your great power
>   and begun to reign.
> The nations raged,
>   but your wrath has come,
>   and the time for judging the dead,
> for rewarding your servants, the prophets,
>   and saints and all who fear your name,
>   both small and great,
> and for destroying those who destroy the earth.
> (Rev. 11:17–19)

God has a response to even the deepest human wickedness and recalcitrance. In apocalyptic thought, when the bas-
tions of goodness seem to have crumbled beyond recognition
or repair, God remains sovereign and thus "a cosmic renewal
occurs, or a golden age arrives, or the earth is transformed into
a paradise."[2]

We frequently limit such apocalyptic confidence to
eschatological visions. While pictures of The End appear often
in apocalyptic literature, we need not wait that long for expressions of confidence that "this is not all there is." On the eve of
his assassination, Dr. Martin Luther King, Jr., preached what
one admirer called his "most apocalyptic sermon"[3] at the Ma-
son Temple in Memphis. At the beginning of that sermon, King
imagined God's asking him to select a time from human history in which to live. After pondering a few options, he said
that he would tell God it would please him to live a few years
in the second half of the twentieth century. Anticipating some
surprise, he explained:

> Now that's a strange statement to make, because the
> world is all messed up. The nation is sick. Trouble is in
> the land. Confusion all around. That's a strange

statement. But I know, somehow, that only when it is dark enough, can you see the stars. And I see God working in this period of the twentieth century in a way that men [*sic*], in some strange way, are responding—something is happening in our world.[4]

King developed that idea throughout the sermon, before bringing it to a triumphant crescendo in the closing paragraph:

Well, I don't know what will happen now. We've got some difficult days ahead. But it doesn't matter with me now. Because I've been to the mountaintop. And I don't mind. Like anybody, I would like to live a long life. Longevity has its place. But I'm not concerned about that now. I just want to do God's will. And He's allowed me to go up to the mountain. And I've looked over. And I've seen the promised land. I may not get there with you. But I want you to know tonight, that we, as a people will get to the promised land. And I'm happy, tonight. I'm not worried about anything. I'm not fearing any man. Mine eyes have seen the glory of the coming of the Lord.[5]

The racial tensions that brought King to Memphis and the social climate in the United States in April 1968 had little resemblance to the glory of the coming of the Lord. But this apocalyptic preacher believed and fervently longed for others to believe in power, goodness, and justice beyond that already seen and experienced. The apocalyptic preacher holds on to the conviction that neither Antiochus nor Caesar and neither the worst that bad people can do nor the best that good people can do limits what can happen. Only God has that power and potential, and the apocalyptic preacher confidently awaits the unveiling of blessings as yet unseen.

After delivering his final speech, Martin Luther King, Jr., did not sit back and wait for the promised land to materialize. Nor did he instruct people to go home and do nothing. The conviction that God can and will unveil power, goodness, and justice as yet unseen must find some way from the heart and soul to the hands and feet. No one can truly embrace that conviction and do nothing. If it is felt, it must be lived. The apocalyptic preacher knows that. *The apocalyptic preacher believes and attempts to help others to believe that what we believe about God should influence, form, and shape what we do and think.* For the apocalyptic preacher, faith is never a matter of simply waiting for an end or even for The End. Faith is a matter of responding to God. Because faith is a verb far more often than it is a noun,[6] "it is existentially impossible to believe in God's coming triumph and to claim [God's] Holy Spirit without a lifestyle that conforms to that faith."[7]

After assuring the believers in Thessalonica that "the day of the Lord will come like a thief in the night" (1 Thess. 5:2), Paul challenges them to live as if they expect this: "So then let us not fall asleep as others do, but let us keep awake and be sober" (1 Thess. 5:6). For Paul, the hope and expectations of his apocalyptic perspective call believers not "to ethical passivity, but to active participation in God's redemptive will."[8] For people who truly believe in a God who reigns as sovereign in the universe, cares for humanity, expands the possibilities of living beyond human limits and abilities, and holds us accountable for our lives, life provides an arena in which to act on those beliefs.

This reflects the heart of apocalyptic thought, but it applies to all attempts to live a life of Christian faith. Belief that God shows no partiality calls for our impartiality. Belief that the power of God finds its fullest expression in love calls for fewer acts of domination and many more acts of compassion. Belief that God hears the cries of the oppressed and promises release calls for our acts of justice and liberation. Belief that God sends the gospel because of our need and not because of our merit calls for nothing less than a reordering of human relationships. The apocalyptic preacher reminds us again and again that when Jesus called for repentance and faith, "he was calling for a new mode of life in view of a new social world on the way."[9] As we trudge from day to day along our journeys in faith, we often start to mouth the familiar words of scripture, creeds, or pious platitudes without reflecting on them or attempting to apply them to our lives. The apocalyptic preacher sounds the trumpet to remind us that believing means responding to God, not merely talking about God.[10]

We must take care not to confuse this clarion call to respond to God with having the responsibility of completing God's work. As Isaiah insists, God's word does not return empty (Isa. 55:10–11). God will accomplish what God sets out to accomplish. Although God may bless humanity with an understanding of the divine will and purposes, fidelity to God means attempting to participate in what God is doing, not doing God's work in God's stead. In Revelation, for example, neither the seer nor the faith community creates the new heaven and earth envisioned in chapter 21. God holds both the seer and the community (along with us!) accountable, however, for preparation for and participation in that new heaven and earth. *The apocalyptic preacher insists that we must measure ourselves by something ultimate.* At any given point in time the faithful can and will lack the ability to thwart injustice, oppression, and hatred. We can, however, believe in, be shaped by, and work for God's vision of justice, liberation, and love. Being people of faith means being accountable to that vision, accepting it as valid and true, and making it the yardstick by which we measure our attitudes and actions.[11]

This represents one of the most liberating, yet demanding, features of apocalyptic thought. When we believe that we have the responsibility of establishing God's realm and completing the ministry of Jesus, the moral and ethical imperatives of the gospel will absolutely suffocate us.[12] Apocalyptic confidence that "this is not all there is" frees us from such impossible obligations. At the same time, it demands faithful stewardship and the use of ourselves and our resources to respond to God by preparing for and participating in what God intends to do and is doing. Apocalyptic thought holds us accountable to God's vision and purpose for creation, the end of things.

We must take care to avoid literalism at this point. Historical annals include myriad tales of groups that have pinpointed a precise date for the coming of the end of time and sought to prepare for it. Apocalyptic thought does not compel us to believe that God moves history toward some single, ultimate, once-and-for-all, catastrophic, and cataclysmic denouement. Some apocalyptic preachers will believe that, and others will not. But whether or not The End is near, there remains an ultimate reality, an end, to which apocalyptic thought holds us accountable. While we may not agree with nuances of her theology, we can find that expressed poignantly in the words of an unschooled but wise woman, who said:

> My Momma told me: remember that you're put here only for a few seconds of God's time, and He's testing you. He doesn't want answers, though. He wants you to know how to ask the right questions. If you learn how to do that, then you'll do all right when you meet Him, and He's there looking you over. You have to tell Him that you've learned how to question yourself, and when you show Him what you know, He'll smile on you. God's smile, that's the sunshine. God's worries, that's the night. We have to face the night. We have to face the end of things.[13]

In the context of this discussion, asking the right questions means holding ourselves accountable to God's will and purposes as we understand them, measuring ourselves not by societal standards of success but by fidelity to the God revealed to us. Since the time is always right for such accountability, the apocalyptic preacher speaks with a sense of exigency: "Keep awake" (Mk. 13:37) and "Let anyone who has an ear listen to what the Spirit is saying to the churches" (Rev. 2:7, 11, 17, 29; 3:6, 13, 22). In every here and now, nothing matters more than God's designs and our faithfulness to them.

This brings us to the theological center of apocalyptic thought for the Christian preacher, who, by definition, considers the Christ-event particularly and uniquely revelatory. For Christians, the life and ministry of Jesus the Christ stand at the heart of everything we know and believe about God. The Christian apocalyptic preacher wants that story told, all of it. *The Christian apocalyptic preacher proclaims the crucified, resurrected, and enthroned Jesus.*[14] Please note the tripartite description of Jesus. No one part of this description will suffice in and of itself.

Only in the complete picture of Jesus do we begin to grasp what God reveals to us, the purposes to which God holds us accountable.

The Jesus of Christian apocalyptic thought is crucified, resurrected, and enthroned. We see this clearly in the vision of the throne room narrated in Revelation 5. In that vision, a heavenly elder assures the seer that only "the Lion of the tribe of Judah, the Root of David" can open the scroll in the hand of God. Then the seer beholds in the throne room "a Lamb standing as if it had been slaughtered." When this Lamb takes the scroll from the hand of God, the heavenly beings twice sing praises that describe the Lamb as worthy because it was slaughtered (vv. 9, 12). Many things in Revelation may not be clear, but this is: The Lamb was slain, crucified. The fact that the Lamb now stands in heaven makes it obvious that he was resurrected as well, and the rest of the book makes it equally clear that God entrusts the control of history to this Lamb.[15] The Jesus of Revelation is crucified, resurrected, and enthroned.

I am stressing this to the point of redundancy because of its theological significance. The Jesus of apocalyptic thought is crucified. The crucifixion indicates that evil is as powerful as it is pervasive. We may want to throw the "blood hymns" out of the hymnal and to keep our crosses golden and pretty, but apocalyptic thought forces us to see, even on the heavenly Lamb of God, the marks of slaughter. This painful sight reminds us of the cost and nature of our salvation. When we refuse to look at the crucified Jesus, we deny both the power of evil and the even greater power of God. In the straightforward and profound words of Fred Craddock: "Churches which try to have Easter without Good Friday are symbolized in the plastic lily: It cannot die and hence it cannot bloom. Resurrection cannot be celebrated if no one is dead."[16] Christian faith does not allow us to escape suffering; it clings to God by a thread called hope in the midst of and despite suffering.[17] That thread expands and becomes a lifeline because this crucified Jesus is also resurrected. God, who is not limited to what we have yet seen and experienced, has an answer for the very worst humanity can do. Just as the death of Jesus "served to reestablish the world *as is*," so does the resurrection of Jesus insist that new realities of God have just begun.[18] We dare to face oppression and rejection because the triumph of the God revealed in Jesus shatters any defeat humans can muster. The enthroned Jesus completes the picture. Authority abides in the Lamb, whom God has led through crucifixion into resurrection. Because of that, as we deal with the challenges of the world we see all too well, we hold ourselves accountable to the purposes of God revealed in the gospel of Jesus. We, like Martin Luther King, Jr., have seen the glory of the coming of the Lord. The details of that glory may not be as clear to us as are those of the world around us, but that does not diminish our confidence that glory will come.

At the risk of further redundancy, I want to underscore the significance of this composite picture of Jesus with a reminder of the Christian assertion that "in him all the fullness of God was pleased to dwell" (Col. 1:19). I say this not to advocate some narrow Marcionite diminishing of scripture and theology, but rather to call for a christology that includes the width and breadth of Christian claims about Jesus. *The apocalyptic Christian preacher relates the figure and the ministry of Jesus as Lord to the ultimate and eternal purposes of God.* Whereas we often attempt to reduce Jesus to a single, dominant characteristic (e.g., love) or a single purpose (e.g., salvation), apocalyptic thought considers him a symbol of the fullness and depth of the mystery of God. In simpler words, apocalyptic thought unabashedly claims that Jesus is Lord, with all the demands that come along with that title and role.

We need that reminder because many of us have become all too comfortable with Jesus! I once shocked several of my students by stating that I would not want to go fishing with Jesus because I wouldn't feel comfortable being that close to him. They were scandalized,[19] and I tried to seize that moment to challenge their christological assumptions. If I had been quicker on my feet, I would have invited them to turn to Revelation and read the description of Jesus to which we referred earlier:

> I saw one like the Son of Man, clothed with a long robe
> and with a golden sash across his chest. His head and

his hair were white as white wool, white as snow; his eyes were like a flame of fire, his feet were like burnished bronze, refined as in a furnace, and his voice was like the sound of many waters. In his right hand he held seven stars, and from his mouth came a sharp, two-edged sword, and his face was like the sun shining with full force. (Rev. 1:13–16)

Looking across the bass boat and seeing this Jesus would make trying to walk on water a distinct possibility!

When we call Jesus "Lord," we do far more than honor him. We declare that he rules in our lives, that his call to us and imperatives for us mean more than those of the would-be lords that beckon us, and that he demands and deserves our allegiance. We cannot shirk his more demanding commandments by standing behind some picture of him as a loving shepherd. We cannot accept the blessings of his ministry but reject his call to discipleship. Because he is Lord, he establishes the ends and purposes to which God holds us accountable. That should not diminish our love for him, but the apocalyptic preacher will insist that it must deepen our obedience to him.[20]

Apocalyptic literature does not limit its shocking pictures to portrayals of Jesus. Quite to the contrary, apocalyptic literature regularly features startling and unsettling images. These word pictures frequently drive away timid readers, but not the apocalyptic preacher, who understands their purpose. *The apocalyptic preacher employs startling and compelling metaphors and symbols that risk offending for the sake of awakening (or revealing).* The apocalyptic preacher operates with the conviction that things cannot and will not continue as they are. The opposition to the church and oppression of the church by cultural and societal norms and mores represent not minor annoyances to the faithful but major threats to the fidelity owed to God. The accountability that the faithful have to the purposes of God represents not an option for living but the only true pathway of life. Yet the church and its leaders all too often lull us to sleep by tacitly or openly depicting the life of faith as something good to do and good for you but not necessarily essential. For fear of appearing conservative or offending someone, many preachers shun firm and clear imperatives and speak only in soft subjunctives and obtuse optatives. The cockcrowing apocalyptic preacher shatters our slumber, more than willing to offend us in order to reveal God's presence and purposes to us.

The final verses of Revelation 19 depict the conquest of the enemies of God. The Word of God presides over this triumph, wearing a robe dipped in blood and wielding a sharp sword that comes from his mouth. According to the vision, he comes to "tread the winepress of the fury of the wrath of God the Almighty" (Rev. 19:15). Assisting him are "the birds that fly in midheaven," who receive an invitation "to eat the flesh of kings, the flesh of captains, the flesh of the mighty, the flesh of horses and their riders—flesh of all, both free and slave, both small and great" (Rev. 19:17–18). The Word throws a beast and a false prophet alive into a lake of fire and slaughters the remaining enemies of God with his sword. The birds fly behind him to gorge themselves on the flesh of the fallen. All in all, this is not a children's bedtime story!

Whereas many preachers prefer to pretend that such images do not exist, the apocalyptic preacher dares to search for their meaning and to employ them for the gospel. One commentator helpfully advises us to find in this scene "not descriptions of real occurrences" but "symbols of the real occurrences."[21] The startling images of the scene alert us to two certainties: First, the awesome powers of evil will fall before the even more impressive power of God, and second, the faithful play no part in this victory. Whether or not we like the symbolism of this passage, it challenges us to have confidence in the ability of God to defeat evil and to identify our task as remaining faithful in the face of evil.[22] Such images are not the only way to convey such a message, but the apocalyptic preacher considers them an effective way. Sometimes we find it hard to believe that God will triumph. Sometimes we falsely think we have to defeat evil for God. Apocalyptic preachers risk making us uncomfortable in order to expel such notions. They have another view of God to advance. They depict a startlingly powerful God, who does for us what we cannot do for ourselves, a God who inspires both awestruck devotion and trembling obedience. Surely we all come to stretches of our journey in faith when that is the image of God we need.[23]

We may need such images from time to time, but that makes them no less unsettling. The apocalyptic preacher intends to disturb us. As already noted, the writers of apocalyptic literature insist that the world cannot and will not continue as it is. The conflict between the ways and rule of God and those that oppose God's ways and dominion has reached a level of intensity that God will not ignore. From the apocalyptic viewpoint, the world that now is will soon no longer be. *The apocalyptic preacher forces a collision between the world that is and a world she or he imagines or anticipates.* In some places, the apocalyptic preacher provides an exaggerated picture of a heinously wicked world and forces the hearer to decide whether or not things truly have become that bad. In other places, the apocalyptic preacher attempts to inspire and comfort the hearers with an idealistic picture of what the world will become. In both cases, the apocalyptic preacher insists that the hearer make a decision. Which will the hearer consider more real, the world of experience or the world envisioned by the preacher?

The vision of the four beasts in Daniel 7 draws such a contrast and calls for such a decision. In the vision, four beasts appear in terrifying succession. The fourth beast "had great iron teeth and was devouring, breaking in pieces, and stamping what was left with its feet" (Dan. 7:7), as it "made war with the holy ones and was prevailing over them" (Dan. 7:21). Only the intervention of God brought these acts of violence to an end. The author of Daniel composed this narrative for the benefit of Jews suffering persecution at the hands of Antiochus IV Epiphanes. The realm of God envisioned in Daniel 7 collided with the experience of the persecuted Jews. The author challenged the faithful to look beyond the historical possibilities and to decide to base their hopes and actions on the world of the vision.

Although some have used such visions and understandings to encourage escape from the world, that is neither the only, the most authentic, nor the most helpful employment of this material. As we read such texts and ponder such visions, we can feel ourselves drawn to make a fundamental decision about who or what we consider most "real." Will we limit our aspirations and expectations to the world we experience or will we believe in and live toward a world envisioned by faith? The apocalyptic preacher insists that we choose one or the other.[24] Even if we do not share that dualistic outlook, we cannot avoid the basic question of where and in whom we will place our faith.

Although individuals must make this decision for themselves, remember that apocalyptic thought focuses on the community more than on the individual. We hear the gospel, encounter resistance to the gospel, and struggle to remain faithful to the gospel in the context of life in community. *The apocalyptic preacher cares deeply about the individual, but insists on addressing corporate and communal good and evil.* Apocalyptic preachers nurture the church, console the church, chastise the church, and hold the church accountable. They challenge the church as a whole to comfort and encourage the faithful, to resist the ways and influence of the opponents of God, and to bear witness to the promises and presence of God that transcend historical circumstances. Although each of us as individuals stand accountable to God, we are neither faithful nor apostate alone. Similarly, the apocalyptic preacher views the evils faced by the faithful as systemic as well as personal. Social structures, as well as individuals, ignore God's ways, threaten the lives of the faithful, and challenge God's sovereignty. That is part of the reason for the emphasis on community. Evil is so powerful that God alone can and will defeat it. While anticipating that victory, the faithful must prepare and respond together.

Please notice that as apocalyptic thought calls individuals and communities to a decision, it places the emphasis on bearing witness to what God has revealed and not on proving the veracity of that witness. The persuasive power behind apocalyptic literature lies not in an appeal to scriptural exegesis or to rational deduction, but rather in the authority of the seer and the revelation received.[25] *The apocalyptic preacher does not attempt to convince hearers that he or she is right as much as the preacher seeks to include the hearer in the unfolding drama of what God is doing in the world.* This does not imply that the apocalyptic preacher has doubts about the revelation received from God or about the message proclaimed to the people. The apocalyptic preacher, however, has a more pressing objective than proving the message. Since human beings can do nothing to hasten or delay the activity of God, the focus is on response. People can either prepare for and, as far as they are able, participate in God's revealed intent or ignore the message revealed to the preacher. Bluntly stated, people can have faith or refuse to have faith. Others may take up the tasks of apologetics; the apocalyptic preacher bears witness and evokes response.

The opening verses of Revelation illustrate this well. They refer to the book as the "revelation of Jesus Christ, which God gave him to show his servants what must soon take place" (Rev. 1:1). They identify the narrator as "his servant John, who testified to the word of God and to all the testimony of Jesus Christ, even to all that he saw" (Rev. 1:2). Then they declare blessed "the one who reads aloud the words of the prophecy" and "those who hear and who keep what is written in it" (Rev. 1:3). The seer has the task of bearing witness and the hearers have the task of responding. As the visions of Revelation unfold, the seer describes, envisions, reports, recounts, and narrates–and in so doing encourages, exhorts, warns, and advises–but does not prove.

Many preachers neglect, forget, or ignore this feature of apocalyptic literature. Some point to modern events and then cite passages that prove that apocalyptic texts predicted them. By proving this connection they hope to convince the hearer to agree with them. Others, many of whom look down their noses at such preachers, avoid apocalyptic material because they cannot pin down the precise message and meaning of its metaphors and symbols. They may not agree with those whom they disdainfully label "Bible-thumpers," but they operate with the same intent. They want to prove the veracity of their message. The apocalyptic preacher challenges us to respond to that which lies beyond proof, to believe what we have yet to understand clearly, to play with an image until it holds us within its grasp and awakens us to unseen presence and possibility, to encounter a mystery so deep that it demands that we be more than we've ever been and gives us hope beyond any we've ever had.[26] The message of the apocalyptic preacher, like nearly every blessing of faith, is too important for proof. It must be accepted, welcomed, and lived.[27]

One final characteristic will complete this description of the apocalyptic preacher. In apocalyptic thought, evil cannot be ignored. The injury inflicted on God's creation and the oppression experienced by those faithful to God defy explanation or comprehension. Yet the apocalyptic preacher is consumed not with evil but with God. Doxologies abound in apocalyptic literature. *The apocalyptic preacher takes sin and its consequences seriously but regularly breaks forth in praise of God.* The apocalyptic preacher lives not only with the nagging certainty that something must be done but also the absolute conviction that something indeed will be done. God will prevail.

Revelation opens with the letters to the seven churches, letters that make the crisis confronting the faithful known. Then, in the fourth chapter, before any trumpets blare or seals are opened, before any descriptions of beasts and dragons, before any account of what has been or what will be, a door in heaven opens and a service of worship begins. Before bearing witness to anything else, the seer portrays the inhabitants of heaven eternally singing:

> Holy, holy, holy,
> the Lord God the Almighty,
>   who was and is and is to come.
> You are worthy, our Lord and God,
>   to receive glory and honor and power,
> for you created all things,
>   and by your will they existed and were created.
>
> (Rev. 4:8, 11)

Such songs of praise frequently find their way into the narrative. No matter how heinous the events described, worship of God continues. In the face of the worst that humanity does and regardless of what humanity does, the worship of God continues. When evil seems invulnerable and when evil lies in ruins, worship of God continues. Apocalyptic thought always offers praise to God.

Although we sometimes treat it as a peripheral or optional activity, worship is essential for a faith community. Worship lies at the heart of who we are. Since we cannot defeat evil, we must depend on God. God deserves worship. Even at our best, we leave something to be desired and we need God. God deserves worship. Ultimately, only God is, only God matters, only God lays legitimate claim on our lives, and only God deserves our allegiance and devotion. The apocalyptic preacher will not let us forget that. Regardless of what is or will be, the faithful have reason to praise God. The apocalyptic preacher will offer that praise whether we do or not.

No sermon on an apocalyptic text will reflect all the characteristics described here. Not every preacher who employs an apocalyptic text will proclaim the gospel. But I hope it has become clear that every preacher that proclaims the gospel owes a debt to apocalyptic thought and can benefit from wrestling with apocalyptic texts. If apocalyptic is "the mother of all Christian theology," there has never been a better time for us to strive to claim our inheritance and become more dedicated daughters and sons.

CHAPTER 4

Daniel 7

Exegesis

Daniel is the only book in the Hebrew Bible whose literary form is apocalyptic. There are other books that employ apocalyptic imagery and participate, at least in part, in apocalyptic's understanding of reality, but only Daniel is a fully apocalyptic writing. Many agree that it is the first Jewish book written in full apocalyptic style. It is also a book that provoked a good bit of interest in the first centuries of its existence. This can be seen not only from the many quotations from and allusions to it in the New Testament, but also by the fact that three additions to it written in Greek are found in the Apocrypha.

The main character of this book, Daniel, is presented as someone who lived during the time of the exile, that is, after the nation of Judah fell and the population was deported to Babylon (today's Iraq). Judah had been a vassal of Babylon since about 605 B.C.E. But when King Jehoiakim saw difficulties mounting between Egypt and Babylon, he declared independence for Judah in 598. He died before King Nebuchadnezzar arrived, but his son (Jehoiachin) was defeated and, along with others of the royal family and leading citizens, deported to Babylon. So the initial wave of the exile began in 597. Jehoiachin's uncle, Zedekiah, was left in charge of Judah and finally was convinced to establish an alliance with Egypt and revolt against the Babylonians in 589. After an eighteen-month siege, Jerusalem fell, and most inhabitants of the city who were left alive were exiled to Babylon in 587. The exile ended when Cyrus allowed the Jews to return home in 538.

While this is the period in which the stories in Daniel are set, this is not the era in which the book was composed. Daniel was written in the second century B.C.E., at the time of the Maccabean revolt. This can be seen from the Greek loan words found in Daniel and from the author's knowledge of the Greek period. His descriptions of events in the period after Alexander the Great, who died in 322 B.C.E., are better than those of the previous Persian and Babylonian periods. The stories contained in Daniel almost certainly existed prior to their inclusion in this book, perhaps even in written form.

The stories and visions brought together in Daniel are intended to help the readers endure the persecution inflicted by Antiochus IV, king of the Seleucid (Syrian) Empire from 175–164/3 B.C.E. Late in 167 Antiochus outlawed Judaism in Judea. He took this step because some of its inhabitants had insistently rejected hellenization, seeing it as a violation of their religion. This religious conviction constantly made his ruling of Judea more difficult. He had tried offering citizenship to those who would hellenize, but the rate of acceptance had been too low. Furthermore, when a rumor was circulated that Antiochus had been killed in a war with Egypt, a rebellion broke out in Jerusalem against the High Priest Menelaus, whom Antiochus had installed. When Roman intervention forced Antiochus to withdraw from Egypt, he marched on Jerusalem. He slaughtered thousands of its inhabitants, reestablished Menelaus as high priest, and stationed troops in Jerusalem. But the trouble did not stop, so in December of 167 he set up a statue of Zeus in the temple of God and sacrificed a pig to Zeus in the temple. Additionally, he outlawed keeping the Sabbath and circumcising children, and he burned as many copies of the Law as he could find. In the following days he decided all residents of Judea should be forced to break the Law. Many were tortured to death rather than deny their faith or violate the Law. Antiochus even sent soldiers to various cities with orders to force everyone, on threat of death, to eat pork. When they arrived in the town of Modin, an old priest named Mattathias killed the first person who was about to take a bite of the pork. He then escaped into the crowd. Our sources indicate that he did this out of his "zeal for the Law." This outstanding deed made him a figure around whom the scattered "pious" could rally. Mattathias died within a year of this act, but his son Judas succeeded him as leader of the movement. Using guerrilla tactics, Judas and his followers retook the temple in three years. Their rededication of the temple to God is still remembered by the festival of Hanukkah.

It is probably after the desecration of the temple by Antiochus that Daniel was written. It was written to help those facing persecution or martyrdom endure. Daniel's stories tell of others who had faced similar situations, who had been ordered to eat unclean food or not to pray to God. When the characters of the stories resist, God intervenes to help them. Such stories were intended to encourage obedience to the Law in those difficult times. Those reading Daniel in the midst of the Maccabean revolt knew that God was not saving their fellows from harm or death, but the stories still brought courage by letting them know that God could (and so might) intervene to save them. It seems that they reasoned that if God was not intervening, there must be a reason, perhaps the previous sins of the people. The visions that begin in chapter 7 of Daniel give another slant on why things were so bad for the people of God. This is an eschatological, apocalyptic explanation. This explanation allows that evil is reigning but asserts that God is about to overthrow that dominion.

The report of the vision in Daniel 7 is given in the first person. This is common in apocalyptic writings. Before this point in Daniel, the stories have been in the third person. So the author of Daniel conforms to the style of apocalyptic writing when he turns to visions. In this first vision, Daniel reports that four beasts rise out of the sea, that realm of chaos which is hostile to God. The four beasts come one after the other and eventually the ruling power of them all is taken away because of the judgment of the Ancient One and by the "one like a Son of Man." The most attention is focused on the fourth beast, who provokes God to action by the arrogant speaking of one of its horns.

Each of these four beasts represents a kingdom. The sequence of kingdoms and kings found here conforms more closely to the biblical accounts of them than to any historical accounts. The first beast is like a lion with eagle's wings. This beast represents the Babylonian Empire. The presence of lions with wings on Babylonian temples and palaces indicates that this is the kingdom the author has in mind. Perhaps its being given the mind of a human alludes to the story of Nebuchadnezzar's being given a human mind after living as an animal for "seven times" (chapter 4). Its wings being plucked may point to the encroachment of the Persian empire on the Babylonian empire. The second beast was like a bear. This beast represents the Medes, particularly in the person of Darius (6:1), who ruled after Nebuchadnezzar. The third beast, which was like a leopard with four heads and four wings, is the Persian Empire.

The fourth beast is yet more terrifying and powerful than the previous beasts. It has no parallel among creatures, with its iron teeth and its crushing of things under its feet. This beast represents Alexander the Great (died 322 B.C.E.) and the empire he established. Alexander's empire encompassed all the other three, which were left as insignificant or as vassals. The ten horns of this beast represent either ten kings within one line (the Seleucids) of the kingdoms that developed after Alexander's death and the breakup of the empire or, as many scholars now think, kings of ten other countries who ruled at the time of Antiochus IV. If this latter view is correct, then the three horns he removes are three kings he defeated in battle. We are not told at this point what arrogant things this horn speaks, but whatever it says provokes God to act, to sit in court as judge.

The judgment scene is a theophany that draws on images of God as warrior and as judge. God's white clothing may point to God's holiness or purity. God's white hair may point to the same characteristics but also to longevity or eternity. The fire that is all about God is a common feature of theophanies in the Hebrew Bible. That the throne is presented on wheels is probably drawn directly from Ezekiel 1. The description of the throne may draw on the image of a war chariot and so further combine God's roles as sovereign judge and warrior. God is also surrounded by thousands of attendants, perhaps pointing to God's majesty, as God enters into judgment.

In God's judgment the arrogant horn is put to death and the other beasts are rendered powerless. But this is not all! The final result is that "one like a son of man" appears in the clouds and establishes the rule of God, which is to last forever. It is interesting to note the contrast between the origin of the beasts and that of the "one like a son of man." The beasts rise from the chaotic and God-opposing sea, while the "one like a son of man" comes from the from clouds of heaven and thus perhaps represents conforming to the will of God. And, of course, the latter is the successful force in the vision.

As one might expect, this vision troubles Daniel, and so he asks one of God's court attendants what it means. He is told that the four beasts represent four kings (v. 17). Here the kings represent kingdoms, just as Nebuchadnezzar represented the kingdom of Babylon in the statue that appeared in his dream in chapter 2 (see vv. 37–38). These beasts are specifically identified as kingdoms in 7:23. Daniel is particularly interested in the fourth beast, especially in the horn that spoke arrogantly. We are given more detail about the activities of this ruler beginning in verse 21, where we are told that he made war against the holy ones and was winning. This condition continued until God intervened in judgment and the kingdom of God was established.

After this brief description of what Daniel saw, a poetic interpretation of the fourth beast and the arrogant horn follows (vv. 23–27). Again the fourth beast is said to establish dominion over all the earth (v. 23). Then the arrogant one arises and we find out more precisely what actions he takes: he speaks against the most high, wears out the saints, and changes the religious calendar and the law (v. 25). Each of these actions, especially the last two, correspond to actions carried out by Antiochus at the time of the Maccabean revolt. The first two are rather general but are certainly appropriate descriptions of the desecration of the temple and the persecution of the faithful. More specifically, Antiochus forbade the observance of Jewish festivals, including the Sabbath, and he tried to put an end to keeping the Law in Judea. We are also told that this horn will be successful at first, in fact, for three and one half years (a time plus two times plus a half time). It is after this amount of time that the Lord will sit in judgment and the horn (Antiochus) will be destroyed and the kingdom of God established (vv. 26–27).

This timetable comes fairly close to describing what actually happened in Judea. The Maccabean forces retook the temple mount in three years and rededicated it to the God of Israel. Antiochus IV died shortly after that. Unfortunately, that did not begin a period of peace because Antiochus V also made war against Judas Maccabaeus and Jerusalem, though he did grant them some religious freedom. After the two-year reign of Antiochus V, the Maccabeans began to gain more political power and religious freedom until ultimately they declared independence for the Jewish state before the end of the second century B.C.E.

This passage, then, speaks to a specific situation in which the faithful of God are suffering persecution precisely because they are being faithful to the Law of God. These were desperate times when faithfulness could entail torture or death, and often did. The situation looked hopeless. The Maccabeans looked impossibly outnumbered and outarmed. What are the people of God to do? What does such a situation say about the power and goodness of God? This vision and its interpretation encourage the readers to remain faithful to God because God will have the last word. God is about to act as judge on those who are persecuting God's people, totally destroying them for their wickedness. Not only that, God will also grant an everlasting kingdom to the people of God. The roles will be reversed so that those now persecuted will reign and those now persecuting will serve those whom they previously troubled. Since verse 27 does not refer to a specific leader, but grants the kingdom to the people of God as a whole, it may be that the "one like a son of man" in verse 13 is to be understood symbolically as the people of God, just as the heavenly attendant calls the beasts kings but means kingdoms. Whether or not that is the case, the point of this vision remains unchanged.

The suffering faithful are assured of the judgment of the perse-cutors and are promised that the power and goodness of God will, in the end, prevail for the good of the people of God. It is important to recognize that all of this activity is presented as an act of God. This is not something the people of God can accomplish on their own. The beast is too powerful for the people to defeat; only God can provide this relief and make these blessings a reality.

Two Sermons on Daniel 7

Few contemporary Christians living in the United States face systematic persecution as a result of their faith. The media regularly ignore or speak disparagingly of the church, and po-litical policies and actions often violate the content and intent of the gospel, but, unlike believers in other places and at other times, our identity as Christians in and of itself does not make us enemies of the state. As noted in the preceding exegesis, the Jews who first heard this text did not enjoy that luxury. Antiochus IV Epiphanes had declared them enemies of the Seleucid Empire. Preachers that want to take this historical context seriously without turning the sermon into a history les-son face the challenge of suggesting ways in which the experi-ences of the second-century Jews intersect with our own. The sermon "Frightful Beasts and Faithful Saints" attempts to do that by uplifting the witness borne by people who remain faith-ful to God in the midst of adversity. Since the Revised Com-mon Lectionary designates Daniel 7:1–3, 15–18 as the Hebrew Bible reading for All Saints Day in the C cycle, I have attempted to link this theme with an understanding of what it means to be a saint.

The second sermon, "Noisy Arrogance and Zealous Hu-mility," takes a different approach to this text and focuses on a specific image repeated within it. On three separate occasions, the narrator describes one of the horns on the fourth beast as arrogant. In the historical situation behind the text, this refers to the callous disregard of Jewish tradition and of the lives of the Jewish people by Antiochus IV Epiphanes. The sermon attempts to identify what makes arrogance not a mere annoyance, but a dangerous and particularly destructive threat to Christian faith.

"Frightful Beasts and Faithful Saints"

Why would anyone compiling a lectionary select Daniel 7 as a reading for All Saints Day? The mention of saints brings to mind the "cloud of witnesses" in Hebrews 12 or, for some, the incense wafting through heaven, symbolizing the prayers of the saints in Revelation 8. But the images of a lion with eagle's wings, a bear with tusks in its mouth, a four-headed leopard, and a ten-horned beast, while possibly appropriate for society's Halloween, seem remote from the church's All Saints Day. As a matter of fact, what are a lion with eagle's wings, a bear with tusks in its mouth, a four-headed leopard, and a ten-horned beast doing in the Bible at all? Such creatures regularly show up on segments of *Xena, the Warrior Princess* or *Babylon 5*, but they seem out of place in scripture. Why would anyone include the likes of these in the Bible and, considering all the possible sermon texts in the Bible, why would anyone choose to preach about them?

Listen to a story, a story from the past that continues to shape our present and possibly, hopefully, our future. Sometime between April and December of 167 B.C.E., Antiochus IV Epiphanes, the insufferably haughty king of the Syrian empire that stretched from modern Turkey south to Egypt, outlawed Judaism in Judea. He prohibited the Jews from reading their scriptures, circumcising their children, and observing their Sabbath. He made it illegal to offer sacrifices to the God of Abraham and Sarah in the Jerusalem temple. To add insult to injury, he sacrificed a pig to Zeus on the altar in Jerusalem and then sent soldiers throughout Judea with orders to compel all residents to eat pork in their presence. The soldiers had orders to execute anyone who refused to eat pork. That left Jews with two alternatives: They could either publicly renounce their faith or die.

When the soldiers reached the village of Modin, approximately a day's journey northwest of Jerusalem, an elderly priest named Mattathias stepped forward to oppose them. According to one legend, he assassinated the Syrian official sent to enforce the orders of Antiochus. According to another, he killed a fellow Jew as he prepared to eat a piece of pork. Whatever the case, Mattathias began a rebellion in which the severely outnumbered Jews drove the Syrians from Jerusalem and rededicated the sacrificial service of the temple. Today the festival of Hanukkah commemorates this victory.

Some might call Mattathias a fanatic. Fanatics do things that don't make sense. Neither risking death rather than eating a pork chop nor killing a neighbor for eating ham makes much sense. Others might call Mattathias a person of conviction, a true believer. He knew in his heart what God expected and attempted to let nothing in his life become more important than being faithful to God. People have been called saints for both reasons.

The story of Mattathias is important because the book of Daniel was written in the early days of the rebellion he sparked. It was written for Jews suffering persecution, who were forbidden to read their scriptures and forced to eat pork or die. The frightful beasts in Daniel symbolize the very real and oppressive foreign armies that had conquered Judea. The last and most frightful beast symbolizes Antiochus with his legions enforcing his blasphemous decrees. The author of Daniel took these beasts seriously. He may even have seen Syrian troops destroying Torah scrolls, terrorizing Judean villages, and executing faithful Jews. But the author of Daniel wrote to encourage the Jews to remain faithful in the midst of this turmoil. He promises that, as powerful as the beasts of Daniel 7 are, they cannot defeat Israel's God. The frightful beasts will rule "for a time, two times, and half a time" (Dan. 7:25), but God promises to destroy them and to inaugurate an eternal kingdom. While admitting that the forces of evil are powerful, he insists that God will intervene for the faithful and that God will triumph over even the most heinous and oppressive evils. The author of Daniel hopes to inspire the faithful to become "the holy ones of the Most High [who] shall receive the kingdom and possess the kingdom forever–forever and ever" (Dan. 7:18). He wants them to keep the faith, to be faithful, to be saints.

It must have worked. Someone saved the stories we know as Daniel, frightful beasts and all! Some people chose to tell these stories to their children, who told them to their children, who told them to their children, who told them to their children in a line that continues to us. Despite the frightful beasts, this story has held meaning for others. What about us? Are there frightful beasts in our world that resemble those in Daniel? If there are, then we, too, can tell the story—frightful beasts and all.

It isn't necessary to start a war to be a saint. It may be necessary, however, to be a little fanatical! Saints believe in God and attempt to be faithful to God even when believing is hard and doesn't make sense. It isn't always foreign armies destroying Bibles and murdering innocent people that make it hard to believe. Challenges to living a life of faith come from a variety of directions.

Sometimes frightful beasts appear in the world around us. When they do, the faithful must believe in spite of them or bow before them.

Betty and John married in the midst of the Great Depression. They owned next to nothing, but that applied to nearly everyone else they knew, so they didn't consider themselves disadvantaged. John worked as a tenant farmer, and since a house, a garden plot, and a few chickens supplemented his salary, they had food to eat and a place to sleep. Betty kept the house, tended the garden, and helped on the farm as often as she could. Her farm work stopped as their five children began to arrive, but the housework increased.

Once on Wednesdays and twice on Sundays, Betty went to church. In the worst of times she took part of her egg money for an offering. That meant a little less fabric for a new dress or a little less spice in the jam cake, but Betty felt thankful for what she had and always made sure to bring something to drop in the plate. Every day began and ended with prayers. One morning John suggested that she could pray and make gravy at the same time. Betty replied, "Man cannot live by bread alone, but the biscuits are on the stove and you can try if you want!" He didn't interrupt her prayers again. As times became better, Betty and John went into debt for a small farm and eventually built a house on it. They were by no means rich, but they were living their version of the American dream.

I met Betty forty years later. By then she came to church only twice each week. Prayer meetings were no longer held on Wednesday nights. She taught a Sunday school class and was the president of a women's circle. She was regularly called on to pray during worship, and whenever she did we received a large slice of our daily bread. I never knew anyone whose faith seemed stronger than Betty's. That amazed me because I knew part of her story. Twenty years before I met Betty, lightning struck her home and burned it to the ground. Before they could finish rebuilding it, John died of a massive heart attack. Three years later, within a five-month span Betty's oldest son died of a massive heart attack and a fire started by a spark from a wood-burning stove destroyed her home a second time. She lacked the financial resources to rebuild and had to sell the farm. I met Betty when I was called to prepare the funeral for her second son, who also died of a massive heart attack. Her instructions to me were simple: celebrate his life.

Betty had reason not to believe. Despite the fact that she attended church regularly, prayed daily, and always shared what she had, she had buried a husband and two children and lost all of her pictures and belongings to fire not once but twice. Misfortune weighed down on Betty. No foreign armies stood at her gates, but she surely felt besieged by frightful beasts. Yet she never missed a service of worship or a Bible study, she placed something in the offering plate every Sunday, and when she prayed the conviction in her voice made everyone feel closer to God. And yes, she was a fanatic. When people took her out to eat, she said grace aloud right there in the restaurant in front of God and everyone. She wanted everyone to know that she loved her God. Some would call her a saint. I do, although I know she would find this embarrassing.

Sometimes frightful beasts show up inside the church. When they do, the faithful must oppose them or join them.

At age fifteen, Connie considered herself ready for motherhood. By the time she was seventeen, she had two sons, no husband, and no high school diploma. It was obvious that her prospects for the future were not good. It was not so obvious that Connie was intelligent, aware of her mistakes, and determined both to provide for her children and to succeed.

Two infants and no money for child care made applying for a job almost impossible. Almost. Some earnest begging convinced a reluctant relative to lend Connie an old car that was one breakdown away from the scrap yard. Having secured transportation, Connie took on two paper routes. The newspaper office delivered the papers to her duplex, where she added the inserts and stuffed them into plastic bags. Then she loaded the papers and the children into the car and ran her routes. Through tight-fisted management of her income, a monthly check from the government, and food stamps, Connie made ends meet and even saved a little.

After both boys had started school, Connie applied for a "real" job on the cleaning crew of the local hospital. The personnel manager scheduled her to work only when her children were in school. After she had put the boys to bed, Connie worked on and eventually completed her high school equivalency diploma. When she drifted off to sleep, she often dreamed of being a nurse. That's when the surprise came. Connie had never been inside a church, so she had no idea what to expect when a social worker said that someone from a local church wanted to make her an offer. The woman said that the congregation wanted to "adopt" Connie. If Connie could pass the entrance exams to a local college, the church would help with her bills and pay her a small stipend for up to five years while she completed her training to become a licensed practical nurse. That fall she started taking large steps toward her dream.

Although the congregation did not require it, Connie thought she should go to some worship services to show them her gratitude. She enjoyed the music and she liked the stories about Jesus told to the children when they gathered at the front of the sanctuary. The rest of the experience was far less pleasant. Every time Connie and her boys entered the building, people stopped talking and started staring. Apart from the Sunday on which the woman who had come to her home sat beside her, Connie sat alone with her sons. One person did walk up to tell her that her boys should go to children's church instead of remaining in the sanctuary. A few people spoke briefly to her at the close of the service before rushing elsewhere. On the last Sunday she came, a woman approached her and abruptly asked, "Honey, is that the only dress you own?"

Connie didn't return to that church. She did complete her training and pass the examination to become a licensed practical nurse. She sent the church a heartfelt thank-you note and promised to try to help someone else like they had helped her. She started attending a church not too far from her new apartment. She waited until her sons were ready, then accepted baptism the same day they did.

Connie had reason not to believe. She lacked the privileges and benefits that make believing in God easy. Although she certainly gained a lot from a church program, her encounters with church people were mixed at best. No foreign armies lined up in her driveway, but Connie probably felt besieged by frightful beasts. Some of them had raised their heads in church! But Connie liked what she heard about Jesus even when the people doing the talking didn't seem much like him. Some might call her a fanatic. Even without a lot of evidence, she believed that Jesus loved her. She still does. We could call her a saint. I do.

Neither a lion with eagle's wings, a bear with tusks in its mouth, a four-headed leopard, nor a ten-horned beast haunts our city streets or country lanes. But equally frightening beasts appear regularly. No one can avoid them. The faithful must oppose them or submit to them.

When someone new arrives at school, all too often a frightful beast named Prejudice roars like a lion as other students taunt her because her skin is a different color or ridicule him because he speaks with an accent. The equally frightful beast called Peer Pressure paces nearby like a lion to make sure that no one befriends the stranger. As government programs allow more of the least of these to slip between the cracks of helping agencies, a frightful beast named Apathy stands menacingly on its hind legs to keep those who could help at a distance.

Another frightful beast called There's Nothing I Can Do growls at those who begin to think they should respond. Similar beasts are as numerous as their names are frightful: Greed, Envy, Jealousy, Bigotry, Lust, Pride, Self-Centeredness, Hatred. Each one stands between the world that is and the gospel's vision of what the world can and should be. Faithful saints, people who hold onto and practice their belief that the love of God makes us all neighbors and keepers of one another, cannot eliminate these frightful beasts. They can, however, by the grace of God, challenge their power by fanatically refusing to bow before them or yield to them. God must do the rest. God will do the rest.

None of this is intended to romanticize or minimize hardships. All of us eventually face times and circumstances that make believing almost impossible. We may not endure systematic oppression and persecution by our government, but we will be ridiculed because of what we believe or suffer a series of accidents and incidents that calls our deepest convictions into doubt. There is nothing glamorous about such frightful beasts. Facing them takes all the courage and faith we can muster. Stories like those of Mattathias, Betty, Connie, and others help us to believe, even when it is hard, that God remains with us and that God will prevail.

Even amid the havoc and destruction of the most frightful beasts we can imagine, God will prevail. No matter what dares to challenge God, nothing can defeat God. Believing this and acting like we believe it can make even ordinary folks like us faithful saints. By the grace of God, may it be so. By the grace of God, so it is.

"Noisy Arrogance and Zealous Humility"

A National Basketball Association millionaire dribbles down the court, taunting his defender with each long and graceful stride. "You got no game, man. You can't handle this. I got every move and you got nothing." He then executes a flawless crossover dribble, pivots, and drives to the basket two full steps ahead of the defender. He scores and the crowd roars. Not content with the points and the accolades, he continues to taunt his opponent, obviously showing off for the television cameras and the fans in the stands. One friend turns to another in disgust and asks, "Can you believe that arrogance?" The reply comes almost automatically, "When you can back up what you say, it's not arrogance; it's just being good at what you do!"

Is that true? When we have superior skills, is there nothing wrong with adding a dose of arrogance while we use them?

An excellent speaker delivers a stirring address. She clearly knows a great deal about her topic, and she just as clearly knows how to speak with passion and conviction. For nearly an hour, she holds the audience spellbound. In the question and answer session that follows, however, she belittles the questioners and offers only condescending comments to honest queries. She obviously feels superior to everyone present. Few would question her knowledge. She is the best in her field. Does that excuse her arrogance?

Arrogance. We see it everywhere. The more arrogant the host of the talk show, the higher the ratings. The more arrogant the commentator, the more games he seems to cover. The National Collegiate Athletic Association has even felt the need to add rules that place limits on celebrations following touchdowns and excellent plays. Are they taking some of the fun out of the game or trying to keep sportsmanship in it? Arrogance. Is it a minor irritation or a major problem?

Arrogance. It seems like a long way from any of the events and circumstances just mentioned in Daniel 7. Daniel 7 describes a surreal world, a world of beasts rising out of the sea and fiery thrones in heaven. But note the description of one of the "characters" that inhabit that world. Ten horns appear on the fourth beast that rises out of the sea. Near the end of the vision, another horn emerges on top of them. A horn symbolizes power. Since this particular horn stands above ten other horns and since all of them appear on a beast described as "terrifying and dreadful and exceedingly strong" (Dan. 7:7), the author obviously considers it extremely powerful, almost too powerful for words. Each time this horn appears in Daniel 7 we discover something else about it, but one particular characteristic appears repeatedly. In the first description in verse 8, the narrator says that the horn has "a mouth speaking arrogantly." Later, when God passes judgment, Daniel reports, "I watched then because of the noise of the arrogant words that the horn was speaking" (Dan. 7:11). Finally, in the interpretation of the vision, the horn is again described as having "a mouth that spoke arrogantly" (Dan. 7:20).[1] Whatever this horn is, more than anything it is arrogant, boisterously arrogant.

Very earthly individuals and situations stand behind the strange images and symbols in Daniel 7. The extremely powerful and boisterously arrogant horn serves as a symbol of the frightening and haughty ruler of the Seleucid Empire, Antiochus IV Epiphanes. The fact that Antiochus chose to refer to himself as "Epiphanes," which we can translate as "the appearance of a god," makes his arrogance clear. Judea was a small territory within the Seleucid Empire. We can easily understand why the Jews would have resented anyone who deemed himself "the appearance of a god." Antiochus' surname, however, was the least of the Jews' problems with him.

Antiochus wanted to hellenize his empire. He wanted all the people he ruled to adopt Greek dress and customs, and he hoped that would bring a sense of unity to the many and varied peoples of his realm. He started by offering citizenship in the empire to all those who accepted hellenization. When many Jews did not respond, however, he turned to more savage methods. He outlawed observing the Sabbath and practicing circumcision. He burned every Torah scroll he could find. He marched into Jerusalem and slaughtered those who resisted him. When Jewish opposition continued, he erected a statue of Zeus in the temple and sacrificed a pig to Zeus on the altar. Eventually, he sent his soldiers throughout Judea with orders to force all the Jews either to eat pork or to die. In his arrogance, Antiochus decided that it was not sufficient to attempt to hellenize Judea; he tried to eradicate Judaism. In his arrogance, he demanded complete submission or death.

I can hear the murmurs now. "Preacher, surely you don't mean to compare trash-talking basketball players and pompous speakers with Antiochus IV Epiphanes! Those are apples and oranges!"

Are they really? Arrogance has a way of festering. All too easily and all too often arrogance transforms mere aggravation into decadent destruction. Arrogance seldom knows when and where to stop. When pride gives way to arrogance, we lose respect for others, ultimately dehumanize them, and treat them with contempt. When feelings of superiority fester into arrogance, we lose our perspective and confuse ourselves with God. That makes arrogance a dangerous, very dangerous, threat to Christian life and faith.

Some people consider their way of life superior to others. That, in and of itself, does not make them dangerous. Adding a dose of arrogance does. When feelings of superiority lead to contempt of others, an innocent man can be brutally beaten and tied to a fence to die because his lifestyle does not measure up. When proud feelings that I am right swell into arrogant insistence that you are wrong, self-professed Christians can show up to picket the funeral of this man who doesn't measure up, adding more pain to his parents' grief. Actions like those threaten Christian life and faith.

When my feelings of self-worth arrogantly deny your worth, that threatens Christian life and faith. When arrogance blindly justifies evil in the pursuit of good, that threatens Christian life and faith. When overactive hubris turns rejection into hatred and one group considers itself above reproach in its dealings with another, that threatens Christian life and faith. When what I assume about the integrity of my convictions makes me presumptuous enough to deny any integrity to yours, that threatens Christian life and faith. Arrogance demeans what God has created, impedes what God envisions for us now, and forever stands between who we are and all that God intends us to become. We do not have to possess either the power or the pomposity of an Antiochus IV Epiphanes to wreak havoc with arrogance in the lives of others.

So what's the good news? This text proclaims the good news that God will not tolerate arrogance forever. The Ancient One on the throne in Daniel 7 takes away the power of all the beasts described in the opening verses, but the fourth beast with its arrogant horn receives particular attention: "I watched then because of the noise of the arrogant words that the horn was speaking. And as I watched, the beast was put to death, and its body destroyed and given over to be burned with fire" (Dan. 7:11). Similarly, the final words of the Ancient One in this chapter single out the fourth beast and its arrogant horn. In the vision God promises the prophet that "his dominion shall be taken away, to be consumed and totally destroyed" (Dan. 7:26). This promise of utter destruction stands in stark contrast with the promise given to those faithful to God:

> The kingship and dominion
>> and the greatness of the kingdoms under the
>> whole heaven
>> shall be given to the people of the holy ones of
>> the Most High;
> their kingdom shall be an everlasting kingdom,
>> and all dominions shall serve and obey them.
>
> (Dan. 7:27)

The arrogant beast has its day, but that day comes to an end. Those who oppose the beast receive a realm that is everlasting.

Is that the way it happened? Did the skies open, release utter destruction on Antiochus and his realm, and inaugurate an eternal Jewish kingdom?

Not exactly. Antiochus did, however, fail in his attempt to eradicate Judaism from Judea. Three years after the desecration of the temple, the Jews recaptured it and rededicated it to God. Antiochus IV Epiphanes died about that time. Faithful Jews still retell that story annually during Hanukkah. The Seleucid Empire remained a threat, but the Jews eventually gained religious freedom and political power. Everlasting dominion did not come to the Jews, but victory over Antiochus IV did.

For us, the issue goes beyond these historical circumstances. For us, the issue is whether we, like the Jews whose faith was threatened by Antiochus, will oppose the threat of arrogance. As the world becomes more and more filled with people and institutions more and more willing to toot their own horns—and to do so with increasingly tragic results—will we both refuse to adopt their methods and openly oppose their designs?

Please notice that Daniel 7 includes many promises for the faithful and that everything they receive in this text comes as a gift from God. In verse 17, the angel tells Daniel, "As for these four great beasts, four kings shall arise out of the earth." Then in verse 18 he adds, "But the holy ones of the Most High shall receive the kingdom and possess the kingdom forever–forever and ever." The beasts "arise," but the holy ones "receive." Similarly, in the closing poetic speech of the chapter the beast devours and tramples as it builds its kingdom, but God gives kingship and dominion to the holy ones.

Anything of value the church has comes from God. Any power the church has, we receive as a gift from God. Any wisdom or insight the church possesses, we receive as a gift from God. Anything that the church has to offer to the world around us–and the church has or should have plenty to offer to the world around us–we receive first as a gift from God. That does not mean that we have nothing to do and it certainly does not excuse slothfulness or laziness on our part, but it does call for humility as we use our gifts.

As society becomes more arrogant, the church can and must proclaim and practice humility. For some reason, humility has a bad name. We often mistake humility for utter submissiveness or spineless docility. We consider the humble wimps, unwilling or unable to stand up for themselves or anyone else. But the truly humble do not acquiesce to every demand put upon them. Instead, the truly humble know who and whose they are. The truly humble may have plenty about which they could boast, but they do not need someone else's admiration or adulation in order to appreciate what they have and who they are. Whereas the arrogant are characterized by what they claim for and about themselves, the humble are known for who and what they serve. All of this makes it possible to be zealously humble.

A zealously humble church distinguishes itself in the community not by its vehement opposition to those labeled sinners, but by its self-sacrificing service in the name of the One who came to call sinners to repentance. A zealously humble church does not passively bow before the oppressor, but aggressively stands up for the God-given rights and dignity of the oppressed. A zealously humble church does not so fear loss of members that it stands in the middle of the road on controversial issues, but rather so trusts in the power of God that it will stand on the side to which God leads it while caring for everyone on that road. A zealously humble church never taunts or belittles another faith community, but always challenges itself and all others to remain faithful to their understanding of God. A zealously humble church gains attention not for the power it wields over others, but rather for the power at work in and through it as it follows its Lord into service of others.

The arrogant cannot curb their appetite for power. Ruling the vast Seleucid Empire did not suffice for Antiochus IV Epiphanes. He wanted to be worshiped as well. Being exceptionally skilled and well paid will not suffice for some people. They want others to bow before their greatness. The arrogant must have someone to stand above. That makes the pervasive presence of arrogance in our society more than a minor annoyance. Arrogance threatens the church and the life God envisions for us. God calls us to follow the One who came to serve into service as keepers of our sisters and brothers, people known by the quality of our caring for all those among whom we stand.

Those who toot their own horns will not disappear. Tune them out, church, for the melody they play has nothing to do with the realm of God. Since their power ultimately fades, they are somewhat comic figures; but the harm they can do before then is tragic. Let us oppose them with all that we have and are. Let us teach our children that no one is exalted by forcing another person to bow. In the midst of noisy arrogance, let us bear witness to a servant Savior. In order to convince the world that nothing we can claim for ourselves compares with the blessings God freely gives to the faithful, let us fill that world with zealous humility.

CHAPTER 5

1 Thessalonians 4:13—5:11

Exegesis

First Thessalonians is probably the earliest written document in the New Testament. It addresses a congregation that was very young and had experienced significant persecution. One of Paul's main purposes in this letter was to provide the young church with an interpretation of their experience that would affirm their Christian faith. The specific occasion of Paul's writing was the return of Timothy from visiting the Thessalonians with a report that they were maintaining their faith, despite the difficult circumstances they were encountering. Paul praises them for their faithfulness, responds to some questions they have sent to him, and comments on some areas in which they need to grow (3:10). First Thessalonians 4:13–5:11 is Paul's answer to some of the questions they have asked. These verses cover two discrete topics: 4:13–18 discusses the place of Christians who die before the parousia,[1] and 5:1–11 deals with the time of the parousia.

1 Thessalonians 4:13–18

Like all early Christians, the Thessalonians believed that the second coming of Christ was very near. The Thessalonians seem to have thought it was going to happen before anyone in their church died. So when some in their church died, they were concerned that those Christians would miss the parousia. Since Paul says he does not want them to have the same grief as those "who have no hope" (v. 13), they may have thought that those who miss the second coming have no afterlife. However, other readings are also possible and perhaps more probable. At the least, the Thessalonians were worried that those who died would miss the blessings associated with the event of the second coming.

As he does elsewhere (e.g., 1 Corinthians 15), Paul begins his response to questions about the resurrection of believers by tying it to the resurrection of Christ. Paul is convinced that Christ's resurrection is the model for and the assurance of the resurrection of believers. Since God raised Christ, God will raise Christians. The point Paul stresses in 4:14 is that the belief that God raised Christ entails the belief that God will raise Christians with him.

In 4:15 Paul identifies what follows in verses 15–17 as a "word of the Lord," that is, as material that the tradition traced back to sayings of Jesus.[2] Many interpreters think Paul is drawing on the same traditions that informed the "Synoptic Apocalypse," especially those used to write Matthew 24, because of the similarities of features and vocabulary. (This book discusses the parallel section in Mk. 13.) It is important to remember that Paul's point is not to set out the exact chronology of all things associated with the parousia. Rather, his main point is to respond to questions about the fate of those Christians who die before it. This is clear from the first words that follow his identification of what he is about to say as a word of the Lord: At the parousia, those living will not precede those who have died. This is the one point of chronology Paul wants to establish.

The imagery Paul uses in verse 16 is commonly found in apocalyptic writings. In this verse he lists three events that are parallel within the structure of this sentence. With this structure Paul presents the Lord's coming down from the clouds, the archangel's voice, and the trumpet of God (these are also found in Mt. 24:30–31) as all a part of the parousia and as happening simultaneously. The only chronological note comes in the last clause of the verse: Christians who have died will be the first to participate in the parousia. According to verse 17, it is only after the dead have been raised and are already with Christ that those who are still alive at the time of the parousia will join Christ in the clouds.

When Paul speaks of those who are still alive at the parousia in verse 17, he uses the pronoun "we." While it is possible that "we" is something like an editorial we, it is more likely that Paul expected to live to see the parousia when he wrote this letter. By the time he writes 2 Corinthians (see 5:1–5) and Philippians (1:19–26) he thinks he may die before the return of Christ. But at this early time he seems to think he will live to see it.

This is one passage from which some readers develop the idea of the rapture. The verb translated "caught up" (NRSV) is the Greek word *harpazō,* which is translated into Latin as *rapere,* the word from which we get "rapture."[3] As a corrective to the ways this is sometimes envisioned, it is important to note that this transporting of the believers into the clouds to meet Christ happens immediately *after* the resurrection of the dead and is part of the one event that is the parousia, the consummation of all things. The taking up of Christians is not a prelude to the parousia but a part of it.

In verse 17 Paul asserts that the final result of all this action is that those who have died and those who are alive at the parousia will, following that moment, be with the Lord always. This foundational belief and trust in the faithfulness of God is what everything else in this passage is built on.

The section ends on a note of exhortation. The portrait of the second coming Paul has sketched is to be used to comfort and encourage those in the Christian community. When we remember that these people are persecuted for being Christians, these words are important as comfort. They assure the suffering that God has not deserted them; and that even death cannot separate them from God and cannot keep God from fulfilling God's loving purposes with them, for God will gather them to God's self forever.

1 Thessalonians 5:1–11

As chapter 5 begins, the broader subject remains eschatology, but the specific topic is now the *time* of the parousia, although Paul has not lost sight of the questions about the participation in it of those who have died. As he did in 4:13–18, Paul sets out his basic response to the issue immediately after stating the question. For anyone who is inclined to calculate when the Day of the Lord will come, Paul responds that it will come when one least expects it. Verse 2 may contain a bit of irony that is lost in most translations. The adverb translated "very well" (*akribōs*) in the NRSV is more literally "accurately," "precisely," or "exactly." So Paul says, "You yourselves know precisely that the Day of the Lord will come like a thief in the night." Just as it seems they know how to calculate precisely when the Day is to come, we find that what they know so exactly is that they don't know. Verse 3 goes on to say that not only will the parousia come when no one expects it, but it will also be sudden. Then Paul adds an ominous and emphatic[4] note: There is absolutely no escape!

It is important to recognize that this warning is not given to Christians, but to "them." This distinction between "them" and Christians is made clear not only by the third-person pronouns (they) in verse 3, but also by the direct contrast with "you" beginning in verse 4. Throughout verse's 3–8 this contrast is stark. There are the children of light and the day opposed to those of darkness and the night; there are Christians and "the rest"; the sleeping and drunk on one hand and the awake and sober on the other. Such clear-cut separations between the people of God and the evil ones are common in apocalyptic. Given that the Thessalonians' experience of the world is one of alienation and opposition, these unmistakable distinctions show that apocalyptic comes from and speaks to those who know just what "Whoever is not with me is against me" (Mt. 12:30) means. There are only two classifications for people within this framework: child of God and child of the devil. There are no other possibilities. Having only these two conceptual categories makes sense of their experience of persecution in a culture that explicitly supports other, contradictory values and uses all the types of powers cultures have to enforce those values. In such settings these drastic contrasts are completely understandable.

Verse 4 not only distinguishes Christians from others, but also says that this sudden and unpredictable coming should not catch them off their guard because they are children of the day and are not in darkness. If taken out of its context, someone might assert that this statement shows that Christians will know when the parousia is coming. But in its context, this is the opening statement in a series of exhortations to watchfulness and self-control. The unpredictability and suddenness of the parousia becomes a reason for always living as one should because Christ may return at any time and without warning.

Beyond the knowledge that the moment of accountability before God may come at any moment, this text supports its exhortation to the moral life by giving the readers a place of high status calling them children of God and then calling upon them to live up to that identity. This is sometimes called Paul's use of the *indicative* and the *imperative*, grammatical terms borrowed to express the relationship between what is and what must be done. Paul often explains who Christians are or explicates some of the blessings they have through the grace of God (the indicative) and then uses those things directly as the bases for ethical demands (the imperative). In this way, the reality of their new existence as Christians who possess God's blessings becomes the basis for the life they must live as recipients of those blessings.

Paul adds here in 1 Thessalonians 5 that since Christians are children of God, God supplies them with the armor that they must put on so they can remain self-controlled.[5] The seriousness of the ethical demands being made on them may be reinforced by Paul's reference to the "hope of salvation," that is, salvation remains in the future and contingent upon their watchfulness. However, immediately after the warning tone is heard, they are offered reassurance; they must be self-controlled because God has set apart Christians for salvation, not wrath. Thus, while their salvation is contingent on their behavior, it is dependent on the will and activity of God accomplished through Christ.

The relationship seen here (5:9) between God and Christ in the work of salvation is precisely the same as was already expressed in 4:14: Salvation is an activity of God that is worked through Christ. What Paul has in mind by saying that this salvation is accomplished through Christ is seen in part in verse 10, where he identifies the death of Jesus as a death "for us." Paul does not explain how this death functions for us but adds only that it is through that death that we will live with Christ. This expression may well point to another way that salvation is accomplished through Christ. Both here and in 4:17 the final state of Christians is "with the Lord/him." Thus, in some way, salvation is life with Christ.

Verse 10 also returns us to the concern that initiated the discussion of eschatological matters, the place of the dead. Paul again asserts that it does not matter whether Christians live until the parousia or die before it; their fate is the same: They will be with Christ.

The final verse of this section, 5:11, states the overall goal of discussing eschatology: The congregation is to use this material to encourage/exhort and build up one another. This was also given as the goal of the section ending at 4:18. *Parakaleō* is used in both 4:18 and 5:11. Sometimes this verb means to comfort or encourage, and other times it means to exhort or urge someone to do something. It seems likely that both aspects of this word are being drawn upon here: The comfort they derive from such reminders is intended to spur them on to faithfulness. This is often a central goal of apocalyptic writings. Here in 1 Thessalonians, the readers are encouraged to be faithful in spite of opposition and persecution, knowing that God is faithful and loving and that God's purposes will not be thwarted in the end.

Two Sermons on 1 Thessalonians 4:13—5:11

As noted in the exegetical comments, the faithful in Thessalonica had become concerned about believers who had died prior to the return of Jesus. Paul, who at this time expected to be alive when Jesus returned, advised them to place their hope in what they believed to be true: the resurrection of Jesus. The God who promised to return Jesus to them had proven able to raise Jesus from the dead. Paul therefore encourages the believers to live lives that manifest their faith and exhibit their confidence and trust in God. The first sermon, "'Caught Up' on This Side of Glory," deals primarily with the closing verses of chapter 4 and focuses on the challenge of remaining faithful to God even when we do not receive the blessings we anticipate. The second sermon, "Too Late to Be a Christian," attempts to respond to Paul's insistence in chapter 5 that since believers cannot know when the day of the Lord will come, they must remain faithful here and now.

"'Caught Up' on This Side of Glory"

If we can believe the story told in Acts 17, it wasn't easy to be a Christian in first-century Thessalonica. Although many residents responded favorably to the preaching of Paul and Silas, and a large crowd gathered at the home of Jason, an early convert, opponents quickly stepped forward to challenge them. What had been a revival suddenly became a riot. The authorities arrested Paul, Silas, and Jason for disturbing the peace. Fearing for their lives, Paul and Silas fled from the city that night. Jason and the other believers, however, remained there. It must have been difficult for them. In the opening of the letter we call 1 Thessalonians, Paul sings the praises of the believers in Thessalonica because "in spite of persecution, you received the word with joy inspired by the Holy Spirit" (1 Thess. 1:6).

"In spite of persecution." No one can say for certain why friends and neighbors persecuted the Thessalonian Christians. Perhaps the believers made themselves unpopular in the synagogue when they ignored long-standing divisions between Jews and Gentiles. Perhaps their strict allegiance to Jesus as Lord sounded unpatriotic in a city that served as a principal administrative center for the Roman government. Perhaps they offended people because of the zeal of their newfound faith. Many of us have had the experience of being turned off by someone who is suddenly turned on. Whatever the case, it wasn't easy being a Christian in Thessalonica. Christians didn't quite fit in with the rest of society and, as everyone knows, those who don't fit in usually find themselves kicked out.

So why bother to be a Christian in Thessalonica? Part of the answer to that question lies in the bonds that formed as believers shared their life and faith with each other. Another part of the answer lies in a promise frequently expressed in Paul's preaching, a promise that sometime soon Jesus would return to earth, assemble the faithful, defeat the enemies of God, and begin a new age of human history. We often refer to that as the promise of the *parousia* or the second coming. In his early days as an evangelist, Paul believed and proclaimed that Jesus would return soon, very soon.

Soon didn't come soon enough for the Thessalonian Christians. When some of the faithful anticipating Jesus' return died while waiting, those who remained started to worry about them. Would they miss the second coming? Had they lost their chance for eternal life? What would become of them?

Paul addresses those fears in our passage. First he reminds the Thessalonian Christians of the cornerstone of their faith: their belief "that Jesus died and rose again" (1 Thess. 4:14). Then he assures the Thessalonian Christians that just as God raised Jesus from the dead, so also would God raise those who believe in Jesus. To that he adds a promise that those who have died will appear with Jesus when he returns in the second coming. At that time the believers who remain on earth "will be caught up in the clouds together with them [deceased believers] to meet the Lord in the air" (1 Thess. 4:17). In other words, Paul assured the believers in Thessalonica that God had everything under control for both living and deceased believers.

Those words may have answered the questions of the believers in Thessalonica, but they don't do a great deal for us, do they? Paul probably wrote this letter about twenty years after Jesus' death and resurrection. Since that time no one has seen Jesus with a host of believers, living or deceased, caught up in the clouds. In fact, many of us feel more than a little embarrassed by Paul's promise. For nearly two thousand years Christians have anticipated the second coming and, as we draw nearer to the year 2000, that expectation has grown, but many of us don't quite know what to say or do about it.

So what should we do? We can begin by stating what scripture and tradition assure us that we do not now and cannot ever know. Whether we call it the *parousia*, the second coming, the Rapture, the Day of the Lord, or the end of time, scripture and tradition insist that we do not and cannot know when it will happen. Paul informs the believers in Thessalonica that, "You yourselves know…that the day of the Lord will come like a thief in the night" (1 Thess. 5:2). In other words, "You don't know when it will happen." According to Mark, Jesus made that even clearer: "About that day or hour no one knows, neither the angels in heaven, nor the Son, but only the Father. Beware, keep alert; for you do not know when the time will come" (Mk. 13:32–33). We can speculate and hypothesize or we can even pass out tracts and pontificate, but we do not know now and scripture says we cannot ever know when Jesus will return.

Does that mean that this passage and its expectations have nothing to say to us? Perhaps not. As we have noted, Paul encouraged the believers in Thessalonica to find and base their hope in what they believed. Can't we do the same? Just as the Thessalonian Christians had their doubts, so may we have our doubts about seeing Jesus and believers (dead or alive) caught up in the clouds together. There remains, however, a great deal that we do believe.

We believe and annually celebrate our belief that in Jesus, God mysteriously mingled divinity with humanity, that in him God somehow took flesh. We also believe that in some way God became manifest in the life and ministry of Jesus, in what he said and did. We do not claim to understand all of that, but we believe that what Jesus did and taught provides glimpses into the ways and will of God. We further believe something almost beyond belief: that when Jesus was crucified, God responded by raising him from death and promising us a share in that victory. We believe that in Jesus, God promises not only not to chain us to the worst we can do but also not to limit us to the best we can do. If we truly believe all or even parts of that, whether or not we are "caught up in the clouds," can't we be "caught up on this side of glory" in what a God this creative and powerful can do?

It wasn't easy being a Christian in first-century Thessalonica. Nor is it easy to be a Christian now. We may not have Paul and Silas running around causing riots in the streets, but we do have a Bible and more than enough teachers and preachers reminding us that Jesus left behind some very hard commands. "Love your enemies, do good to those who hate you, bless those who curse you, pray for those who abuse you" (Lk. 6:27–28).

There are other commands, but those will suffice. Who can possibly do that? We prefer keeping score, getting even, and watching out for number one. If we didn't, people would take advantage of us, run over us, and humiliate us. Imagine a world in which we tried to take care of people who do not care about us. Imagine a world in which we didn't keep score. Imagine a world in which we acted with love whether or not we received it. What kind of world would that be?

Yes, God says, please do just that: imagine what kind of world that would be. Imagine a world in which people of faith truly tried to bless the lives of people expecting nothing but a curse. Imagine a world in which followers of Jesus spent their time and energy not in keeping score but in trying to make sure everyone got a chance to play the game. Imagine a world in which believers tried more to make friends than to keep enemies. None of that would be easy! If we did that, it would be only by the grace and with the help of God. Yet isn't that exactly what we are promised? Isn't that precisely what the grace and help of God do in us and for us?

God, working in Abraham Lincoln, helped him to discover that we lose our enemies when we make them our friends. Haven't we been blessed when we tested that idea and found it true? God, working in and through Martin Luther King, Jr., helped him to pray for those who stood in his way as well as for those who marched beside him. Although we still have a long way to go, isn't that the reason we've traveled this far? God, working in each of us, has helped us to experience that it is easier to let go of a grudge than to hold onto it, that it is harder to hate someone whom we have held by the hand, that it is easier to love someone for whom we have prayed by name. Hasn't God helped all of us to do something we once thought impossible? When God has done that, when God has helped us to do what we never imagined we could do, didn't we feel "caught up on this side of glory"? Don't we feel that way even now as we remember those moments?

It wasn't easy being a Christian in first-century Thessalonica. The Christians there found themselves out of sync with their friends and neighbors. When we practice our faith, truly practice our faith, it isn't easy being a Christian now either. As Walter Brueggemann suggests, in many ways we are exiles living in an increasingly secular world, a world that does not share our values and priorities.[6] In this world that draws so many lines of distinction, our belief in a God who shows no partiality often makes us shout, "Measure people by the quality of their character and not by their tennis shoe manufacturer!" In a world infatuated with comfort and convenience, we who believe that God calls us to take up our crosses daily must insist that anything of value demands something from us. In a world that has less and less patience with those in need, our belief that God shows preference to the poor calls us to sometimes extravagant acts of generosity and compassion. As we do this, the world complains, "That doesn't make sense!" and we respond, "Being faithful to God is more important than making sense!"

And it is, isn't it? Isn't being faithful to God wonderfully more important than making sense? Every congregation at some point in time has ignored the skeptics and offered help not because someone appeared to deserve it but because he or she obviously needed it. Regardless of what the odds-makers might have said, didn't it feel good to bring fresh potential to a stale situation? We all have heard of inner-city congregations that decided to remain there and change the focus of their ministry rather than move to what the experts call a more suitable location. Didn't the story of their courage and conviction warm our hearts and inspire us? Some of us have attempted to make our congregations and services of worship less homogeneous. We have sung songs by Amy Grant and Andraé Crouch alongside those of Fanny Crosby and Charles Wesley. We have allowed the hands passing our offering plates to become white and black, female and male, aged and youthful, callused and smooth. We have made room intentionally for people we once excluded unintentionally. Hasn't that diversity blessed our lives and experiences? Haven't we been "caught up on this side of glory" in the strange and gracious joys of belonging to a community that ranks being faithful to God above making sense?

It wasn't easy being a Christian in first-century Thessalonica. Jesus didn't return as soon as they thought he would. We know something about that. We have not yet seen him riding a cloud in the air! For believers then and now, salvation and the realm of God–however we define them–don't seem to materialize instantaneously. After nearly two thousand years of Christianity, we still face some of the same problems. People, good people, people of faith, still die daily. Some of them die painfully, slowly, or tragically. Illnesses and injuries wreak havoc on a regular basis in the lives of believers. We pray, we worship, and we live as faithfully as we can manage, but we see little, if any, improvement. Sin remains as strong and as prevalent as ever. In fact, many of us fear sin may be getting stronger! Why, after nearly two thousand years, are things still so difficult?

That "why" leads to another "why" that is even more painful. Since things remain so much the same, why continue to believe? Why hold on to our crumbling faith? Why continue to expect Jesus to come?

Why? The simplest answer to that–which is by no means a simple answer–emerges from who we believe God is. We believe that God will be God regardless of what does or doesn't happen. We believe that nothing in life or death can keep God from caring for and being with those who believe. We believe that God will keep God's promises. And God does.

Nearly every Sunday for the last thirty-three years, I have gathered with believers somewhere to receive the loaf and cup. On many of those occasions, the preparation for the meal has included the words, "For as often as you eat this bread and drink the cup, you proclaim the Lord's death until he comes" (1 Cor. 11:26). In those thirty-three years, I have yet to see Jesus and a group of believers (living or deceased) "caught up in the clouds together." Nor have I heard others say that they have witnessed such a sight. But on the first Sunday after my father's death, in those moments of silent remembrance at table, I felt strangely close to him. On the Sunday following the Oklahoma City bombing, at table many received solace that they found unavailable elsewhere. When the week brings us more than we think we can possibly bear, the simple act of receiving the loaf and cup more often than not brings renewed strength to tired faith. During those times when no answer comes to even our most fervent prayers and we feel frighteningly alone, God draws near in communion. The bread of heaven and the cup of salvation are not fast food. They offer no instantaneous cure for what ails us and no quick fix to our brokenness. But as we receive them, we often find ourselves "caught up on this side of glory" in the mysterious and gracious presence of God.

The world can be cold, hard, and demanding. Compared with most, we are people of wealth, privilege, and prosperity; but the world remains cold, hard, and demanding. Acts of nature can devastate us and human nature can leave us in despair. For people with no faith, the realm of possibility is no larger than their own capability. They cannot hope for anything greater than their own best efforts. How can anyone live like that?

We don't have to live like that. We believe in a God who can mingle divinity with humanity. We believe in a God who can raise the dead. We believe in a God who can triumph over the very worst we can do. We believe in a God who can bring even greater potential to the best we can do. We believe in a God not bound by our limitations, a God whose creativity and love exceed all expectations. With a God like that, who knows when we'll next find ourselves "caught up on this side of glory"!

"Too Late to Be a Christian"

Freddie was different. My high school classmates and I never talked about it or analyzed it, but we all knew that Freddie was different. Freddie never joined us for sandlot baseball or driveway basketball games. In fact, he participated in sports only when the coach forced him to during gym class. I don't remember Freddie's ever speaking during a classroom discussion. When he did talk, he lowered his eyes and mumbled. It took effort to hear and understand him, effort we rarely exerted. He belonged to no clubs and took part in no extracurricular activities. Whether the crowd numbered three or three hundred, Freddie could and did get lost in it. I'm sure he had talents, but we never saw them. Nor did we look. We all knew Freddie, but it would be a stretch to call us his friends.

I never thought about it, but Freddie must have been lonely. How terrible it must have felt never to be noticed, or only teased on those rare occasions when someone did pay attention. School teachers and church youth group leaders tried to teach us better, but we never applied those lessons to Freddie. We never did anything especially bad to Freddie; but we didn't do anything particularly good for him either. We left him in the dark. One could even say that we were darkness for him. Looking back, it seems strange that it shocked us when he disappeared. What did we expect or encourage him to do? After he was gone, it was too late, too late to be a Christian.

At the end of chapter 4 and the beginning of chapter 5 of 1 Thessalonians, the apostle Paul addresses a specific concern raised by the community of faith in Thessalonica. Like all early Christians, the believers in Thessalonica expected the second coming of Jesus to occur soon. In fact, they appear to have thought that this would take place before any of their church members died. That obviously didn't happen. Some of the remaining Christians feared that those who had died would miss Jesus' return. Paul begins his response by assuring them that they need not "grieve as others do who have no hope" (1 Thess. 4:13), because when Jesus returns "the dead in Christ will rise first" (1 Thess. 4:16). Then he addresses a more pressing concern. Since "the day of the Lord will come like a thief in the night" (1 Thess. 5:2), the Christian community could not predict when it would occur. They could, however, prepare themselves by living up to their status as children of God until Jesus returned: "[Y]ou are all children of light and children of the day...since we belong to the day, let us be sober, and put on the breastplate of faith and love, and for a helmet the hope of salvation. For God has destined us not for wrath but for obtaining salvation through our Lord Jesus Christ" (1 Thess. 5:5, 8–9). In other words, regardless of when Jesus returned, the present was the time to live their faith. Those who did that would have nothing to fear. Those who did not, those who "fell asleep," faced the possibility of finding it too late to be a Christian.

It isn't hard to fall asleep. It can happen before we realize it. We don't always choose darkness; we simply forget to act like children of light.

The world moves quickly and we move rapidly in it. We seldom have or find enough time to do what we feel we must do. That leaves even less time for what we think we should do. We have the best of intentions, and we know all too well the cliché about them and why that has become a cliché.

We truly mean to teach our children to pray. We do manage to help them to learn a simple table grace, but little more. Then we turn around and they have become teenagers or they've left for college. How did that happen? It's late. Is it too late?

We honestly meant to visit a long-cherished friend. We even drove past the house on several occasions, but it never seemed like a good time to call. Then we picked up the paper and read the obituary. We fell asleep and now it's too late.

Every day for two weeks we read the advertisement asking for volunteers for the adult literacy program. Teaching an adult to read would be both challenging and rewarding. It might even help someone to get a better job. We find reason after reason for not getting involved and excuse after excuse for putting off the phone call. Oh well, someone will do it. We fall asleep and, for us, it's too late.

Every year during the annual congregational meeting, we squirm in our pew as Grumpy Gertie and Cynical Sam lament the demise of the church and lambaste the leadership of the congregation. We want to stand up and tell them what we think. We want to draw some attention to what we think is going well. We want to say a good word for those who work so hard and give so much. But annual congregational meetings last too long as it is, so we remain silent. We might as well sleep. Again this year, it becomes too late.

Recognize the scenario? Feel the guilt?

Don't we all? We all know that we regularly fail to do the good we intend to do. We all fall short of the goals we set for ourselves. If being a Christian means being awake, then we confess that we spend a lot of time asleep. Then we worry about that as well. What must God think about people like us? What will become of people like us? Is it too late for people like us? That all depends. Hear again the words of Paul:

> Now concerning the times and the seasons, brothers and sisters, you do not need to have anything written to you. For you yourselves know very well that the day of the Lord will come like a thief in the night. When they say, "There is peace and security," then sudden destruction will come upon them, as labor pains come upon a pregnant woman, and there will be no escape! But you, beloved, are not in darkness, for that day to surprise you like a thief; for you are all children of light and children of the day; we are not of the night or of darkness. So then let us not fall asleep as others do, but let us keep awake and be sober; for those who sleep sleep at night, and those who are drunk get drunk at night. But since we belong to the day, let us be sober, and put on the breastplate of faith and love, and for a helmet the hope of salvation. For God has destined us not for wrath but for obtaining salvation through our Lord Jesus Christ, who died for us, so that whether we are awake or asleep we may live with him. Therefore encourage one another and build up each other, as indeed you are doing. (1 Thess. 5:1–11)

Just as it wasn't too late for the Thessalonian Christians who had died to meet Jesus, neither is it too late for us. Today is the time to claim and manifest our identity as children of the light. God, in Jesus, has prepared the way. We need only travel it.

There is no shortage of disasters in the world. Honduras and Nicaragua have yet to recover from Hurricane Mitch, but some in the National Weather Service already have predicted increasing hurricane activity throughout the next decade. Week of Compassion, Church World Service, and other helping agencies seldom lack reasons to call for our help. Each time the destructive forces of nature flay some community somewhere, it is time to be a Christian. We can't fix everything, but we "put on the breastplate of faith and love" (1 Thess. 5:8) and turn a check or a blanket offering into a helping hand that lets others know that someone cares and that they are not alone. Who knows—once we've done that for a while we might even work ourselves up for a mission trip!

We need not look to distant lands or across the nation for such opportunities. Nearly every community has a soup kitchen or a food pantry. Some also have a homeless shelter or a ministry to transients. All communities include children to befriend and people who need help with odd jobs or small chores. We may have passed such people daily for years, but now remains the time to show that "we belong to the day" (1 Thess. 5:8). None of us can be all things to all people, but each of us can be something to someone. We could even volunteer at the hospital or hand out sandwiches on a cold street corner as a family. When we keep awake, we can always find a good time to be a Christian.

Look around the sanctuary. If all of us took the time and effort to turn one or two acquaintances into friends, what new life might pulse in the congregation? Look around again. Who's missing? What difference might a card, a telephone call, or a brief visit make? Look around again. Surely somewhere there is an overworked volunteer in need of an hour or two of help or a small task a couple of us could have fun doing together. Even without hearing "the archangel's call and...the sound of God's trumpet" (1 Thess. 4:16), can't we tell that it is time to be a Christian?

No, we cannot do everything. Yes, there will always be more assistance needed than we have the time and resources to provide. No, we are not responsible for everyone. We are, however, accountable to God. As children of light, God fills us with the capacity to care and the desire to make a difference. It is up to us to use those gifts, to find time to be a Christian.

As the year 2000 approaches, a lot of people are making a lot of noise about "the day of the Lord" and encouraging us to get ourselves right with God before it is too late. Paul adamantly declares that we know very well that all we can and do know about that day is that it will come unexpectedly. Whatever it is and whenever it comes, doesn't God actively participate in our lives right here and right now? Doesn't God constantly and in many and various ways guide us, warn us, rescue us, challenge us, console us, and call us? If God still does all of that, is it too late to be a Christian?

I live with the awareness that a day came in my relationship with Freddie when it was too late to be a Christian. I have asked for God's forgiveness, and I believe that God has granted that forgiveness. But I would prefer to avoid many more days like that. I say that not because I fear hell and not because I have convinced myself that I can become perfect. The forgiveness and grace of God make perfection unnecessary and the threat of hell innocuous. I would prefer to avoid many more days like that because I have seen the power of the light and I'd like to be a child of the light. I've seen hands of hope lift up those crushed by despair. I've heard words of faith transform dead ends into new beginnings. I've witnessed a small act of love illuminating the deep darkness of hatred. I'd like to be a part of that and something tells me that it is not too late.

God knows there is plenty of darkness in the world. God alone can drive out that darkness forever. God promises to do precisely that. But what might happen if fewer of us waited until it was too late to shine in the darknesses we encounter? Imagine what kind of world that would be. Imagine how it would feel to live in a world like that.

By the grace of God, we are much more than we give ourselves credit for being. By the grace of God, there is much much more that we can become. "For God has destined us not for wrath but for obtaining salvation through our Lord Jesus Christ, who died for us, so that whether we are awake or asleep we may live with him. Therefore encourage one another and build up each other, as indeed you are doing" (1 Thess. 5:9–11).

CHAPTER 6

Mark 13

Exegesis

Mark 13 is often called the "Synoptic Apocalypse." It has long been the subject of controversy because of its treatment of the fall of the temple and the end of time in a single passage. To understand this passage well we need to examine both its literary form and its place within Mark.

In form, this chapter is more like a testament than other forms we find in apocalyptic writings (e.g., a vision). This form is known from works written both before and after the writing of Mark. The Testament of the Twelve Patriarchs[1] contains several examples of this genre. These Testaments contain what is presented as some of the last words of these people of faith, though they were written centuries after these people had died. Such works reveal the theological and eschatological views of their later authors. Their primary concerns are things happening in the time of the actual writer, which are often addressed by presenting the issue in the form of predictions made by those who lived long ago. Mark presents the remarks of Jesus in chapter 13 as some of the last things Jesus says to his disciples before his death. Furthermore, the subject of this discourse, the fall of the temple, was an important matter for all Christians when Mark was written.

Mark was written sometime just before or just after the fall of the temple in Jerusalem. This was a traumatic event for both Jewish and Gentile Christians. Jewish Christians had continued to worship in the temple until its destruction (see, e.g., Acts 2:46 and 21:17–36). Gentile Christians also knew it as the only temple of the true God they had begun to worship. So what are they to think when this temple is destroyed? Does it mean their God is not as powerful as they thought? Does it mean God rejects the Jews? What could this mean about use of the Hebrew scriptures, the only Bible they had? How could the God of the whole cosmos allow the one temple dedicated to that God to be overrun? Does it mean that things have gotten so evil that the second coming of Christ is imminent?

Mark 11:11–13:37 is dedicated to interpreting the fall of the temple. Chapter 11:12–26 combines what is usually called Jesus' "cleansing of the temple" and the story of the cursing of the fig tree with a literary device known as intercalation. This device puts together two stories that are to be interpreted as a single unit.[2] The combination of these two stories shows that Mark does not see Jesus' actions in the temple with those selling animals for sacrifice and the currency exchange brokers as a cleansing of the temple, but rather as the closing of the temple. That is, Jesus declares that the temple's time has passed. Just as the cursed fig tree was out of season, so now the temple's season has passed. This understanding of Jesus' actions at the temple would help Christians cope with the fall of the temple because it tells them that it has less significance than they were attaching to it. With these episodes Mark is asserting that Jesus recognized that the temple would fall soon and had himself initiated its closing.

Chapter 12 contains Jesus' exchanges with those in charge of the temple. Mark portrays them as insincere and dishonest. This supports Mark's position that the temple no longer functioned as the place of the special presence of God and thus its fall is not so devastating for Christians. Following his exchange with these leaders and his comments on their insincerity, Jesus leaves the temple for the last time. As he does, his disciples look back and comment on how large and magnificent the temple is. Jesus' immediate response is that the temple will be destroyed (13:1–2). This response causes the disciples consternation, but it should also function as a source of encouragement for Mark's readers, who have now experienced its fall (or know that it is about to fall). It should provide some comfort to them to know that, even before his death, Jesus knew this was to occur. So the question of whether the destruction of the temple is devastating for Christian faith has been addressed, but the question that remains is: What does the fall of the temple *mean*? Does it have eschatological significance? Mark 13 addresses this question.

Mark says that when some of the disciples were alone with Jesus, they asked him two questions about his prediction of the destruction of the temple: When will it happen? and What will the signs for it be? Jesus responds to the questions in reverse order but answers neither. Instead he addresses the time of the end. Verses 5–27 talk about signs of the end, while verses 28–37 deal with the time of the end.

Chapter 13:5–8 begins Jesus' response. These verses describe the time of the Roman war in Judea (66–70 C.E). The time described in these verses is a time of war, famine, and earthquake. It is the kind of situation in which Christians hope for the direct intervention of God and look for the presence of God in some overwhelming manifestation. These verses intimate that in the context of the terrible destruction brought by this war, some people had arisen claiming to be the messiah ("Many will come in my name and say, 'I am he!'" [v. 6]). Perhaps they were Christians or people who appealed to Christians claiming to be the returned Messiah/Christ. Jesus exhorts these disciples not to believe in such people because as terrible as the Roman war would be, it was not a sign that the end was near—it was only the beginning of the birth pangs (v. 8). So the first answer to the unasked question about signs of the end is that the Roman war was not one of them. Some writers suggest that this rejection of the Roman war as a sign that the end is near was intended to cool eschatological enthusiasm among Mark's readers. At the least it says that this event, though seen by some as such, was not an indication that the end is near.

Verses 9–13 turn to the subject of persecution. From the earliest days of Christianity, persecution had been seen as a sign that the end could not be far off. After all, if God is to remain just and loving, God must intervene to stop the pain of those who suffer because of their belief in God. Mark has Jesus predict that Christians will be handed over to all kinds of judicial officials and bodies. Jesus does not say God will spare them, but rather that God will be with them in the midst of these persecutions. God's Spirit will sustain them through legal examination and probably torture, helping them to maintain their confession and express their faith so that they do not have to worry about what to say in defense of their faith.

These verses also indicate that the lives of these Christians will be patterned after Jesus' life in some significant ways. Not only will they be persecuted, but just as Jesus was, they will be betrayed by those close to them. Some interpreters think Mark is here referring to those Christians who have been betrayed by other Christians. It is possible that some had betrayed fellow believers to escape death or torture or because of theological differences. Whether such betrayals were occurring, we do not know, but Mark's community has experienced persecution and probably the betrayal of some members by people close to them.

This section may also intend to quell immediate eschatological expectations by saying that the gospel must be preached throughout the whole world before the end comes (v. 10). It is doubtful that this had been accomplished by the time Mark was written. The section ends by asserting that those who endure the persecution with faith will be saved. Thus, it is an exhortation to faithfulness in the face of persecution. However, it does not make these persecutions a sign of the end. If anything, it puts off the end by requiring the gospel to be preached to all nations. So for the second time Mark has Jesus reject the notion that something that might well be seen as a sign of the end, and probably had been understood as such, was in fact a sign. Rather than looking for the immediate end, they are to endure with faith.

Verses 14–23 turn attention back to the temple. This has often been seen as one of the most difficult sections of Mark 13 because of its enigmatic imagery and seemingly threatening tone. But if we remember the historical and literary context of Mark, it is less difficult. The first image in these verses that needs our attention is the "desolating sacrilege" or, as it is better known from the King James Version, "the abomination of desolation." Perhaps the first thing to notice is that Mark expected his alert readers to recognize this figure (or object) almost immediately. That is the meaning of the parenthetical remark, "let the reader understand" (v. 14). As in all apocalyptic texts, such imagery is used to point to persons or events that readers could recognize and identify. While the meaning of this symbol may have been clear to Mark's initial readers, it has been the object of much consternation and speculation since then. This is often the case because interpreters of this passage have sought to identify this person with someone in their own time in history rather than in Mark's time. But for this passage to be meaningful to Mark's readers, it had to be someone they knew, so it *must* refer to someone in the first century.

This "desolating sacrilege" is an image drawn from Daniel (9:27; 11:31; 12:11—the phrase "let the reader understand" is also a way to direct the reader's attention to this literary allusion). In the context of Daniel it refers to Antiochus IV Epiphanes (who ruled Syria around 175–164/3 B.C.E). Antiochus defiled the temple by erecting a statue of Zeus in it and sacrificing a pig to that god in the temple. This desecration became a paradigm for those who would defile the temple or hinder Jews from practicing Judaism. The works that record the conflict between Antiochius IV and the Jews of Judea (1 and 2 Maccabees) are in the Septuagint. This Greek translation of the Hebrew Bible was the most commonly used version of the Bible among early Christians. So when this image from Daniel is brought into Mark, the readers understand that the subject is the temple—especially the desecration of the temple. The two first-century options that seem most likely are the emperor Caligula and the Roman general (later to be emperor) Titus. In 40 C.E., Caligula decided to press the matter of emperor worship in Judea by erecting a statue of himself in the Jerusalem temple and having sacrifices made to him there. He was persuaded not to carry out this course of action, and his four-year reign ended the next year. Thus, the temple was not actually defiled.

The second and more probable option for identifying the "desolating sacrilege" is Titus. Titus was the son of Vespasian, the general in charge of the Roman army in Judea during the war, which took place in 66–70 C.E. While the war was in progress, Vespasian perceived that if he were to return to Rome he could seize the position of emperor. He left for Rome to secure that position for himself and left his son Titus in charge of the war. Titus completed this task, including the siege and destruction of Jerusalem and the temple. Since he directed the destruction of the temple, he seems to be the most likely candidate. So verses 14–23 are about the destruction of Jerusalem and the temple in 70 C.E.

The description of the difficulties those in Jerusalem will have to endure during this time is frightful. Verse 19 again draws on Daniel (12:1) when it describes this time as the most difficult in the history of the world. The tribulations are so great that no one would survive except for the mercy of God, which is issued on behalf of Christians to reduce the time of this terrible suffering. In these desperate circumstances, Mark's Jesus predicts again that people will appear claiming to be the Messiah (vv. 21–22). These false messiahs will be so convincing, Mark says, that even some Christians will be tempted to follow them. But Mark says all such claims are to be rejected. So the terrible destruction of Jerusalem and the temple are not signs that Christ is returning. The false messiahs who even perform signs may say this is the time of the presence of the Messiah, but Jesus says in advance that it is not because the fall of the temple is not a sign of the end.

This passage does, however, give instructions about how to react to these times. In verse 23, the disciples are told to "be alert." This may have a double meaning. First, they need to be alert about the coming of the destruction of Jerusalem so they can escape it, as verse 14 tells them to flee to the mountains. But perhaps more importantly, this is an eschatological warning that calls on them to be alert about the real second coming and to be alert so they are not deceived by the false messiahs.

Mark has now had Jesus say that the Jewish war, persecution of his followers, and the destruction of Jerusalem and the temple are all *not* signs of the second coming. Finally, in verses 24–27, Jesus turns to the end itself. This is to happen sometime after all the suffering associated with the fall of Jerusalem. These verses say that the coming of the Son of man will take place in conjunction with cosmic portents. This is probably a way of saying that the whole of creation is involved with the coming of the Son of man. This is not an event about which anyone will need to be told because everyone will see the Son of man coming in the clouds and all the elect will be gathered to him. This ingathering of the people of God is probably seen as the fulfillment of the promises of God made to those in exile (see Deut. 30:4; Isa. 11:11, 16; 27:12; Ezek. 39:27). This event is the opposite of the scattering of the exile; it is the reclamation of the people of God for God. So the coming of the Son of man, as it is envisioned here, will be seen by all and will achieve the purposes of God.

Now if we return to the question: "What are the signs?" we still have no answer. The only sign that the end is coming is that the end begins. None of the things others had designated as signs that the end must be near are accepted as genuine signs. They are, rather, explicitly rejected as signs. So as Mark closes this discussion of the signs of the end, his message has been that there are no events in world history one can point to as clear evidence that the end is near. Not even the destruction of the temple is such a sign.

After Mark concludes that there are no certain signs of the end, he turns to the subject of the time of the end (vv. 28–37). In this section Jesus tells two parables and offers some comments on them. The first of these, the parable of the fig tree, compares the coming of the Son of man to the sprouting of the fig tree in summer. When we see the leaves coming out, we know it is summer. Again the point seems to be that there is no time to look for signs. When you see one, the time is upon you. Verse 30 adds urgency to this matter by saying that these things will all happen during "this generation." The "all these things" clearly refers to the coming of the Son of man as well as the destruction of Jerusalem and the persecutions. We know from our vantage point that the end did not come in the first century, or in the time of that first generation of Christians. Perhaps Mark intends "this generation" to refer to his readers rather than the generation of the apostles, but that does little to resolve the problem. Verse 32 may help us understand this passage a bit better. Verse 32 asserts that no one knows the time of the end except the Father; not even Jesus knows. If this is the case, how can Jesus assert in verse 30 that the end will happen in "this generation"? There is a tension between these two verses that can be important for maintaining an apocalyptic perspective. It is important that the end is soon ("in this generation") and that its exact time is not known. These two points together call on the readers to be in a constant state of readiness for the second coming. And that is the point emphasized in the following parable of the man who goes on a trip and leaves his slaves in charge of the household.

This second parable is introduced with the exhortation: "Beware, keep alert." The parable then goes on to say that the servants must constantly be ready for the master's return because they do not know when he will return. The parable is followed immediately by the exhortation, "Keep awake." So rather than giving a timetable or giving a list of signs to look for, Jesus tells the disciples to be ready always because the end will come suddenly. So Mark has moved the emphasis from the end coming quickly to the end coming *suddenly*. This is a subtle but very important shift. It turns one's attention away from trying to predict when the end will come to living in a constant state of readiness for it. Because the end will come suddenly, one must always keep her/his accountability to God in clear focus.

Mark wants to be certain that his readers understand that the exhortations drawn from these parables are as much for them as for the disciples on the Mount of Olives. So Jesus' last sentence in this discourse is directed not to the disciples, but to the readers of Mark: "What I say to you [the disciples] I say to all: Keep awake." Thus, Mark's readers are exhorted to be ready always for the sudden coming of the Son of man.

Mark 13 has taken us on a circuitous route. It begins with the prediction of the destruction of the temple, moves to the question of when that destruction will happen, then to discussion of the things that are not signs that the end is near (including the destruction of the temple), to comments about how sudden the end will be, and finally to an exhortation to always be ready for that sudden end. This passage accomplishes at least two functions in Mark. First, it completes Jesus' dealings with the temple, showing that its fall is no surprise and that it is not a portent of the end. Furthermore, the fall of the temple is not to be construed as a sign of God's weakness because it was known to Jesus and Jesus himself had announced the closing of the temple (chapter 11). Second, chapter 13 leads to the same goal we find in much apocalyptic writing. Its rhetoric, which culminates by designating the end as sudden, is designed to exhort the readers to constant faithfulness in the face of persecution and the fall of the temple.

Two Sermons on Mark 13

Every third year, many preachers groan when they note the gospel reading for the First Sunday in Advent. The B Cycle of the Revised Common Lectionary lists a section of Mark 13 as the gospel reading for that day. Some preachers sigh when they notice that the prescribed reading omits Jesus' prediction of persecution for believers and the ominous description of "the desolating sacrilege" (Mk. 13:14), but sufficient challenges remain for those addressing parishioners who make little distinction between Advent and Christmas and forget that the "sweet little Jesus child" grows up to become the powerful "Son of man." What do heavenly portents, the gathering of the elect, and a slave owner coming home unexpectedly have to do with our preparations for Christmas? The first sermon on this text, "Keep Awake," attempts to respond to this challenge. It is intended to help a congregation begin its journey through Advent.

As the year 2000 approaches, more Christians will discover or turn to Mark 13 and ask their leaders what these verses mean. Many religious leaders in the surrounding community will stand more than willing to answer their questions. The second sermon, "We'll Know He's Coming When We See Him," attempts to respond to both some of the questions posed by the faithful and some answers to those questions that many of us find irresponsible and damaging to the life of faith.

"Keep Awake"[3]

Late in the autumn of 1990, a scientist predicted that a major earthquake along the New Madrid Fault would shake the ground from western Kentucky and Tennessee southward to the Mississippi Delta. Seismologists have discussed the possibility of such an earthquake for decades, but this prediction attracted an unusual amount of attention because it designated a specific date: Tuesday, December 4, 1990. By December, few newscasts, public assemblies, or private conversations in the area failed to mention the predicted tremors. People stowed away precious possessions, stockpiled groceries and kerosene, and learned how to shut off their gas and water lines. Schools and businesses announced that they would be closed that week and several residents temporarily left the area. Attorneys stayed busy as hundreds of people wrote their wills and "put their affairs in order." On December 2, 1990, the First Sunday in Advent and two days before the predicted quake, churches were packed. The mood neared panic. Many people stayed awake all night on December 3, some of them in churches holding candlelight vigils.

December 4, 1990, passed with no tremor. December 1990 came and went with no shaking of the earth. Winter turned to spring without seismic upheaval. Flashlight batteries drained. Extra food spoiled or was consumed. Fuel tanks sat empty once more. Only trained professionals continued to conduct disaster drills. Church attendance and life returned to normal. Sleep once again came easily. When a crisis seems imminent, we have no trouble keeping awake. When the threat of danger seems remote, our eyelids grow heavy and we sleep.

When Mark composed his Gospel, many Christians expected the messiah to return to earth at any moment. Indeed, many would-be messiahs appear to have declared that they had already arrived! Many believers considered the words "Truly I tell you, this generation will not pass away until all these things have taken place" (Mk. 13:30) a hard and fast promise that Jesus would soon return to establish the realm of God on earth.

The time certainly seemed ripe for the divine intervention. Relations between the Romans and the Jews soured daily. By the time Mark wrote his Gospel, Roman legions probably had begun their long and devastating siege of Jerusalem. In fact, that siege may already have ended and Jerusalem may already have lain in ruins. To make matters worse, relations between Jews and Christians were moving from disgruntled tolerance to hostile rejection. Add to that double-digit inflation and frequent food shortages and we easily understand why many of the faithful felt certain that a day of divine intervention had drawn near.

Nearly two thousand years have passed since Mark composed his Gospel. We have yet to see "'the Son of Man coming in clouds' with great power and glory" (Mk. 13:26). Few of us here expect to witness such an event. Some of us have little patience with those who do. Others of us do not know what to make of predictions of a bodily return of Jesus to earth. Even talking about it makes us uneasy. God knows we have seen myriad military crises, natural disasters, and economic downswings, and the advent of the year 2000 certainly has prompted a flurry of predictions of the end of the world. A new one glares at us in the supermarket checkout line every week! But isn't such talk mere fanaticism?

Our uncertainty over what to do with apocalyptic visions and predictions of the end of time do not give us permission to roll over, go to sleep, and ignore this text's and Advent's call to "keep awake." "Keep awake!" Those words apply to far more than preparation for and anticipation of cosmic upheaval and cataclysmic destruction. They call us to awareness of the fact that God holds us accountable for what we do with our lives. "It is like a man going on a journey, when he leaves home and puts his slaves in charge, each with his work, and commands the doorkeeper to be on the watch. Therefore, keep awake" (Mk. 13:34–35). In other words, whether or not it makes us feel comfortable, God expects something of us. Grace is free, but it is not cheap. We cannot earn a relationship with God, but it costs something to have one. God's involvement in our lives does not make us puppets. We have decisions to make, important, life-changing decisions. Jesus comes that we may have life and have it abundantly, but he does not force that life on us. He offers abundant life to us and we must decide whether we want it and whether we will accept it. We must decide.

Because the church relies on volunteers and often seems meek when competing with other demands on our lives, we easily drift into a casual approach to and attitude about who and what we are as people of faith. We go to sleep. This text and the season of Advent sound the alarm, "Keep awake!" They alert us to the fact that God entrusts us with sacred tasks.

At times all of us think we would like to see "the sun... darkened...the stars...falling from heaven, and the powers in the heavens...shaken" (Mk. 13:24–25). We would like to witness an unquestionable and irrefutable sign that God is alive, powerful, and at work in the world.

Such signs come. "Keep awake!" Our faith challenges us to discover the presence, power, and ministry of God arriving and unfolding through us and in us, as well as around us and for us.

A group of central Kentucky youth jettison their spring break plans for a trip south to Florida and instead travel west for several hours to spend a week stacking sandbags for people they have never met previously and probably never will meet again. During one of the busiest times in the year, church members add to their already extensive shopping lists the names of people they do not know and purchase presents they will not see opened. Someone with a longer "to do list" than anyone could do stops at an extended care facility and slowly feeds an aging friend. A person with no answers to give invites a co-sufferer first to lunch and then to a worship service. Such actions do not shake the heavens—or do they?

"From the fig tree learn its lesson" (Mk. 13:28). Because we have received love, we have the responsibility and the opportunity to love. Because grace has touched us, we have the call and the potential to touch others. Because we have been given worth, we have the commission and the capacity to impart worth. Because week after week we come to the table as beggars and receive the loaf and cup, we have the mission and the possibility of preparing the way for other beggars to be fed.

"Keep awake!" Perhaps our churches do not ask enough of us. Perhaps our clergy fear offending us and soften the claim God and the gospel lay upon our lives. Perhaps our lay leaders do not make our involvement in congregational life and ministry seem critical. Perhaps we have a thousand feelings of inadequacy or impotency. None of that changes anything and all of that changes nothing. The challenge remains. "Keep awake!"

At times all of us feel like praying with Isaiah, "O that you would tear open the heavens and come down, so that the mountains would quake at your presence...to make your name known to your adversaries, so that the nations might tremble at your presence!" (Isa. 64:1–2). We want the evil to know that they defy not only human standards but also divine dictates. Evil can appear so prevalent, so potent, and so predominant that we feel utterly helpless and hopeless. We fall asleep.

"Keep awake!" The justice of God works through us and in us, as well as around us and for us.

A Caucasian woman ignores the scornful glances and disapproving stares to have lunch with an African American classmate because she values principle above popularity. Busy people take the time to teach an adult to read because they know that the battle against poverty is waged with their presence as well as their words. A concerned teacher in desperate need of her salary puts her career on the line and files a report when the bruises on a child from an influential family look suspiciously unlikely to have come from "a fall." Such actions do not cause the earth to tremble–or do they?

"From the fig tree learn its lesson" (Mk. 13:28). Because we belong to the Prince of Peace, we have the call and the potential to be and to become peacemakers. Because the God we claim and who lays claim to us loves justice and kindness, we have the responsibility and the opportunity to defend the innocent and to protect the powerless. Because our God shows no partiality, we have the commission and the capacity to confront prejudice and oppression.

We may not feel comfortable in such roles. We may not feel equal to such tasks. We may not want to take such stands. We may prefer to close our eyes and sleep. None of that changes anything and all of that changes nothing. "Keep awake!"

This may sound like too much. There is more. The season of Advent and this text seek not only to awaken us to our call and potential, but also to open our eyes to what God does in our midst. Sometimes the earth quakes and the heavens rumble, but most of our experiences of God are not that dramatic. God doesn't just move mountains; God moves hearts. God doesn't just part the waves of the sea; God crushes the barriers that keep neighbors apart. God doesn't just raise the dead; God enlivens the living.

The season of Advent declares the mystery of incarnation, God choosing to mingle divinity with humanity. Advent declares that God does not have to disrupt the natural order to be with us, because God is with us in the natural order. The promise, "Where two or three are gathered in my name, I am there among them" (Mt. 18:20), is not an excuse God gives us with which to console ourselves when attendance is low. It is a gift we receive from a God who chooses to participate in our lives, all of our lives. In the sanctuary we do not merely worship God. We commune with God. We do not merely serve God. We work with God.

We do not have to wait until the end of the world to know God. Our relationship with God is not something we achieve by or at the end of life. Our relationship with God is something we discover in the midst of living. Divinity mingles with humanity suddenly and often where least expected. "Keep awake!" Expect to hear prophetic words from the lips of a child. Anticipate receiving vision from eyes dimmed by age. Prepare to sense the sacred in the presence of a stranger. Get ready to feel strangely warmed in the commonplace and customary.

It is not easy to keep awake. Some fall asleep during worship every Sunday. Children leap from eight to eighteen. Marriage covenants dissolve into contracts. Friendships fade into acquaintances. Shining hopes lose their luster and become shattered expectations. In the bliss of joy, the boredom of the commonplace, and the numbness of disappointment, we sleep. We sleep.

"From the fig tree learn its lesson" (Mk. 13:28). No matter what falls or fails—even the temple and the church—all around us are people in whom to see Christ and to whom to bear Christ, people to forgive and people from whom to receive forgiveness, people with whom to form the realm of God and people in whom to discover the realm of God. That hour and that time can and do come suddenly, unexpectedly, at any time.

"Keep awake!" That is a jarring command, because there is so very much to do. "Keep awake!" That is a gracious invitation, because there is so very much to see. "Keep awake!"

"We'll Know He's Coming When We See Him"

According to information found while browsing the Internet, a series of events that will lead to the parousia, the second coming of Jesus, has already begun. Those events started, of course, in 1998. Why 1998? Basic math makes it elementary. As everyone knows, chapter 13 of Revelation identifies 666 as the most evil number, the number that symbolizes the antichrist. And, as everyone also knows, three is one of the perfect numbers. When we multiply three times 666, we get 1998, the perfectly obvious year of the antichrist!

According to another source, scientific data supports this conclusion. A solar eclipse occurred in South America in February 1998 and meteorites showered the earth during November 1998. Those events fulfill Jesus' words:

But in those days, after that suffering,
the sun will be darkened,
    and the moon will not give its light,
and the stars will be falling from heaven,
    and the powers in the heavens will be shaken.
(Mk. 13:24–25)

The weather in 1998 provides even more convincing evidence. Remember the hurricanes and volcanic activity of 1998? Remember how meteorologists attributed that and a variety of peculiar weather patterns to something called El Niño? Well, El Niño means "little boy" and refers to "the Christ child." We experienced a destructive weather pattern named "The Christ child." We all can recognize that as another sign of the antichrist, using Christ's name but opposing his nature.

This and other evidence make it clear that the antichrist has begun his final quest for earthly dominion. The time has come for people to choose either to bow before him or to accept the real Christ. Jesus will return soon, very soon, to defeat evil and begin his eternal reign.

According to Damian Thompson, religious affairs correspondent for *The Daily Telegraph*, some people are more prepared for this than others:

> In no place on earth is the Second Coming of Christ awaited with such desperate yearning as Seoul, South Korea. Every night the city skyline becomes a litter of red neon crosses, each of them representing a community of born-again Christians…But the crosses are not there to commemorate the earthly Jesus of Nazareth: they are runway lights to guide in the airborne Christ the King who, when the great predestined moment arrives, will appear on clouds of glory to inaugurate the Millennium.[4]

At least he will know where to land!

As we not so slowly move toward the year 2000, similar predictions of and preparations for the second coming and the end of time appear almost daily. They glare at us from tabloid headlines in the grocery store checkout line. They shout their warnings on predawn television programs and late night radio. They come from a variety of sources and they draw on an impressive array of scriptural passages and scientific data. In the midst of all the clamor they raise, confusion they cause, and consternation they generate, what's a Christian to do?

At the risk of sounding like yet another raving fanatic or biblical fundamentalist, I want to make a suggestion. Why don't we do what Jesus advises us to do in Mark 13? "But about that day or hour no one knows, neither the angels in heaven, nor the Son, but only the Father. Beware, keep alert; for you do not know when the time will come" (Mk. 13:32–33).

Many biblical scholars refer to Mark 13 as "the Synoptic Apocalypse." The chapter opens with Jesus and his disciples exiting the temple in Jerusalem. The disciples, most of them backwater Galileans, behave like typical tourists. They strain their necks and hold their mouths agape, while staring at the sights of the big city. As they marvel at the temple, Jesus says:

"Do you see these great buildings? Not one stone will be left here upon another; all will be thrown down" (Mk. 13:2). Only after they travel from the temple to the Mount of Olives do the disciples muster the courage to ask Jesus what he meant by that. Jesus then addresses the destruction of the temple and "the Son of Man coming in clouds" (Mk. 13:26).

Hearing Jesus address such issues piques the interest of nearly any Christian, but the initial readers of Mark probably raised their eyebrows farther and more quickly than we do. Mark was written either shortly before or shortly after Roman legions completed their siege of Jerusalem and destroyed the temple. Jewish and Gentile Christians surely gasped as one. How could the only temple of the only God fall? How could the God of the messiah allow such a catastrophe and all the suffering related to it? Had the world become so wicked that Jesus must and would return soon? So again we ask the question: What's a Christian to do?

Note first and foremost that Mark's Jesus does not equate the fall of Jerusalem with "the end." "Beware that no one leads you astray. Many will come in my name and say, 'I am he!' and they will lead many astray. When you hear of wars and rumors of wars, do not be alarmed; this must take place, but the end is still to come" (Mk. 13:5–7). The fall of Jerusalem, although devastating, is not "the end." Jesus then declares that Christians will suffer in many and various ways. After this he repeats his warning: "And if anyone says to you at that time, 'Look! Here is the messiah!' or 'Look! There he is!'–do not believe it. False messiahs and false prophets will appear and produce signs and omens to lead astray, if possible, the elect" (Mk. 13:21–22).

Then Jesus offers a simple truth surrounded by two parables. First the parables. "From the fig tree learn its lesson: as soon as its branch becomes tender and puts forth its leaves, you know that summer is near. So also, when you see these things taking place, you will know that he is near, at the very gates" (Mk. 13:28–29). In other words, when summer arrives, that's when we know that it is summer. Now the second parable. "It is like a man going on a journey, when he leaves home and puts his slaves in charge, each with his work, and commands the door-keeper to be on the watch. Therefore, keep awake–for you do not know when the master of the house will come, in the evening, or at midnight, or at cockcrow, or at dawn" (Mk. 13:34–35). In other words, when the maid and the butler see the limousine coming up the driveway, that's when they know the homeowner has returned. Now the simple truth: "But about that day or hour, no one knows, neither the angels in heaven, nor the Son, but only the Father. Beware, keep alert; for you do not know when the time will come" (Mk. 13:32–33). How much clearer could he make it? We do not know and we cannot know when Jesus will return! Even *he* doesn't know! Since even he doesn't know and we do not and cannot know, he gives us this advice: "Keep awake!" We will know that he is coming when we see him!

Keep awake! However, wherever, and whenever Jesus returns, he calls us now, where we are and as we are to live lives of faith. Jesus challenges us not to prepare for the second coming, but rather to be prepared for it. Jesus instructs people of faith not to get ready to awaken in a moment, in the twinkling of an eye, at the sound of the last trumpet, but instead to keep awake until we hear that trumpet sound. The second coming, however, whenever, and whatever it is, is Jesus' promise that in every here and now of our lives God holds us accountable for vigilance in our faith.

Back in the days when I worked for a living, I spent a little time in charge of quality control at a milk processing plant. I had the task of making sure that we stayed in compliance with the standards set by the health department. We were inspected on a regular basis, but we never knew on what day or at what time the inspector would come. Many longtime employees had elaborate theories about when the next inspection would occur, but those predictions failed even more often than their picks for the winner of the game of the week! Basically, we knew when the health inspector would come when we saw his truck pull onto the parking lot. If we had waited until then to put ourselves in compliance with the health codes, we would never have stayed in business. Although I took pride in what I did and wanted to maintain a clean plant and to produce a safe product, I confess that it didn't hurt to have an utterly unpredictable inspector hold me accountable.

I can already hear the complaints of many sophisticated, contemporary Christians, especially those that often consider faith an option more than an imperative and those that regard Jesus primarily as a benevolent but benign teacher. "That sounds like a threat, preacher! You're trying to frighten us into faith!" To the charge of thinking that God in Christ expects something from us, I plead guilty. I firmly believe, first, that both we and the world belong to God, and second, that God has something invested in how we use our lives. Such convictions can prove more than a little frightening, but not nearly as frightening as believing that God does not exist or that we have no one but ourselves to whom to turn for help and hope. I consider it good news that we have a God and a savior who care enough to become involved in our lives—even if we cannot know when the Son of man will come until we see him coming.

But the good news doesn't stop there. Note the limits placed on what God expects of us. Mark 13 insists that we bear witness, endure, and keep awake; but it does not make us responsible for creating or building the realm of God on earth. Instead, like slaves in charge of the home while the owner takes a journey, God holds us accountable for the tasks entrusted to us. God in Christ does not hold us responsible for the success of the gospel in the world. Instead, God in Christ holds us accountable for bearing witness to the Christ we follow and for manifesting our faith in the way we live. That is the work God has given us until the end comes.

When will that occur? When will Jesus return? Remember what Jesus said! We do not know and we cannot know. Only God knows. We will know that he has come when we see him. But we can agree with the people predicting his imminent arrival about one thing. The time certainly seems ripe for Jesus to return!

Following Hurricane Mitch in November 1998, devastating mudslides buried towns and villages in Honduras and Nicaragua, killing more than eleven thousand people and inflicting intense suffering on countless others. In that same month, poor people died daily in Russia as the coldest winter in thirty years descended on a people already besieged by shortages of food, fuel, and medicine. When we think about these situations we cringe; yet we know that they are not isolated. Natural disasters magnify the suffering of the least of these on a regular basis. Now would be a good time for Jesus to return and bring harmony to creation.

Two days after Thanksgiving in 1998, the seventeen-year-old captain of a Louisville, Kentucky, high school football team died needlessly. Multiple gunshot wounds in the back ended Adrian Smith's life and his dreams of playing college football. He was not a part of the argument or whatever it was that led to the gunfire. He had the misfortune of innocently stumbling into the confrontation. He probably didn't know who shot him or why.[5] The story breaks our hearts. It comes close to breaking our spirits as well, because in our violent and gun-filled society innocent people die daily. On high school campuses, in the streets of Beirut, on country lanes, and in nearly every isolated and populated dot on the globe, we slaughter and sacrifice each other to violence on a regular basis. Now would be a good time for Jesus to return and put an end to our warring madness.

When the end does come, in a moment, in the twinkling of an eye, someone will set up a stand and start selling T-shirts. If the second coming takes more than a day or two, fast food restaurants and souvenir shops will appear as well, closely followed by a tennis shoe company waving a contract for a limited edition of "Son of Man High-tops." With only a few shopping days left until the end of the world, demand will drive prices as high as the cloud on which Jesus stands! That's the way we are. We're consumers. We consume and consume, yet never quite fill our emptiness. We spend so much time preparing to purchase that our spirits become as empty as our purses. Now would be a good time for Jesus to return and teach us the difference between having things in abundance and having abundant life.

When will Jesus return? We will know he's coming when we see him. Until then we have some work to do.

We cannot stop hurricanes and natural disasters. We cannot put back together again all the pieces of the lives they break.

Such ministry belongs to God alone. We are not responsible for making everything right; but we are accountable for how we respond. We can keep and practice the faith: organizing mission trips; collecting outreach offerings; praying daily; caring for others because we have both the capacity and the command to do so. Strangely, as we do our work, we receive as well as impart blessings.

We cannot put an end to all human violence. We cannot melt every icy heart of hatred, prejudice, bigotry, apathy, and meanness. Such ministry belongs to God alone. We are not responsible for eliminating the senseless acts of violence that plague humanity; but we are accountable for how we respond. We can keep and practice the faith: kneeling in grief-struck prayer beside the victim; standing to confront and to pray for the offender; confessing our own violent tendencies and seeking healing; searching for and practicing ways of resolving conflict in which no one loses; caring for others because we have both the capacity and the command to do so. Miraculously, as we do our work, we receive as well as impart blessings.

We cannot alter all global, national, and local economies. We cannot eliminate all the longing to possess and all the insecurities that drive our rampant consumerism. We cannot even help everyone to see how one person's insatiable longing for more means less for several others. Such ministry belongs to God alone. We are not responsible for repairing all the damage done; but we are accountable for how we respond. We can keep and practice the faith: consuming less so that others will have more; becoming as aware as possible of the price others pay for our purchases; taking time to notice and give thanks for richness that has nothing to do with possessions; learning to want to have less so that we can give more; caring about the ways our lives affect others because we have both the capacity and the command to do so. By the grace of God, as we do our work, we receive as well as impart blessings.

If Jesus returned and found us doing all of this or even trying to do all of this, what would he think? He might think that we were afraid he would catch us asleep, but it seems more likely that he would think we actually believe in him. He might think our faith kept us awake! Imagine that. It might surprise him so much that an angel would have to keep him from falling off his cloud!

When will Jesus return? We do not and cannot know. So we don't have to worry about it. In fact, as 2000 approaches we can sit back and have some fun watching people pretend to know more than they do. While we watch, we can keep awake, keep awake for opportunities to practice our faith. There will be plenty of them. When Jesus returns, we'll know he's coming when we see him. Until then, we can live in him even before we see him coming. By the grace of God, may it be so. By the grace of God, so it will be.

CHAPTER 7

Revelation 5

Exegesis

The book of Revelation has been both one of the most popular and most frightening books in the canon. It has spoken to many groups and been understood in very different ways. As with the other passages we have examined, the first task is to locate this document in its own time and to try to understand its message in that context. So we begin with what we can know about the historical setting of the writing as a whole.

Revelation was written by John, a Jewish-Christian prophet who was familiar with the congregations of western Asia Minor (today's Turkey). There is no evidence in the text that would lead us to identify him with the apostle John. So this writer's authority did not come from a claim to apostolic office, but from the recipients' knowledge of him as a prophet and from the medium of the writing, an account of a revelation from God. Revelation is usually dated in the reign of Domitian (81–96 C.E.). It is often asserted that there was a severe persecution of Christians during this time and that Revelation is a response to that persecution, which included the exile of John to Patmos. However, there is almost no evidence outside Revelation that there was a systematic, empire-wide persecution of Christians during this time. Still, Christians of Asia Minor did live under the threat of persecution, as the exile of John himself indicates. Even without broad governmental and violent persecution, Christians faced many things they interpreted as persecution and as the work of Satan.

The more common sort of persecution first-century Christians seem to have faced was economic and social. This sort of persecution should not be seen as trivial or as less difficult to endure than our usual conception of persecution as something that involves physical torture or death. This latter kind of persecution is brutal and painful, but swift. Persecution in the form of economic disadvantaging and of being treated as a social outcast is something that must be endured constantly. It is not just a matter of standing bravely for your faith one time, but of having to question your commitment to Christ in the face of continual difficulty and pain inflicted on both yourself and your family. Most early Christians were from among the lower reaches of society, a society in which there was almost no middle class. Before becoming Christians, most of these people survived on a subsistence level with little or nothing left over for anything that was not a necessity (e.g., most people in this class almost never ate meat). After their conversion to Christianity, things probably got worse for them, because becoming a Christian meant that they were expected to forgo certain activities which disadvantaged them economically.

A good example of this is their attendance at trade guild meetings. Groups of people who worked at the same trade in a city would sometimes meet together to discuss business, perhaps go together to purchase supplies in bulk, and engage in other business-related activities. Unfortunately for Christians, these meetings were often held in dining rooms connected to or associated with temples of various gods. Early on Christians began arguing about whether it would be acceptable for them to attend these meetings, eat the dinner (some of which had been offered in sacrifice to the god of the temple), and so participate in the business-related activities conducted there. In 1 Corinthians 8–10 we find that some Christians thought attendance at such meetings was acceptable as long as the Christian did not participate in the worship of the other god and as long as the Christian understood that the "god" being worshiped by the others was not truly a god. But Paul rejects this line of argument, asserting that Christians were not to be part of these gatherings—both for their sake and that of other

Christians who might not know that other gods are not real
gods–because they may be tempted to believe in those gods
again. Revelation takes up this same issue in its letters to the
churches (chapters 2–3). John also demands that Christians not
compromise with the world by partaking of food sacrificed to
idols (see, e.g., 2:14).

This issue was more important than it may sound. It was not
just a minor inconvenience. Participation or nonparticipation,
particularly if it were known that one's absence was for religious reasons, may often have been the difference between
having enough to eat and going hungry. Think of the trial to
your faith it would be to send your children to bed at night
knowing that they were hungry because you were a Christian.
This is a genuine and very painful type of persecution, as real
as any violence one can envision.

Socially, Christians' nonparticipation in various civic activities was required by their commitment to worship only the
one God. They would be viewed as unpatriotic and just strange
if they did not participate in the cult of the god of their city or
take advantage of gifts sometimes distributed by temples. Again,
one's whole family would suffer because of this faith. Being an
outcast voluntarily is a difficult role to play for one's whole life,
but that was what was required of Christians in this period.

So whether the persecution of the Christians who received
Revelation was from Domitian or from the more common experiences of Christians, their perception was that the world
was against them. As they interpreted their experience of reality, it seemed obvious that Satan was in control and doing all
in the power of Satan to make things difficult for Christians.
Their experience, then, brings to the surface the questions that
apocalyptic writings usually address. They need a word of hope
about the victory of God and about their participation in that
victory. If we remember that the earliest Christians believed
that the end was very near,[1] the difficulties the recipients of
Revelation faced are made even more difficult. Approximately
sixty years had passed since Christians first began to proclaim
that the second coming was near, and perhaps the expectation
of the end was waning among some groups. If that was the
case, then there was no prospect of relief from the difficult

circumstances in which they lived. Revelation renewed that hope, saying that the end was near, even if not as soon as most had thought. Thus, they were exhorted to remain faithful and detached from the world and its advantages.

The primary purposes of Revelation, then, are to assure those who are suffering that God will set things right and will do this soon, and to exhort them to faithfulness, given the certainty and swiftness of this action by God. All the strange (to us) imagery and numbers contribute to those purposes. The imagery was not intended to be literal or difficult. That the symbols are not to be understood literally can be seen from passages such as 17:1–14, where John interprets the image, thus giving us a key to how to read other material in the book. This passage, which identifies the scarlet beast and the great prostitute as the Roman Empire, also shows that the imagery of this book is focused on people and events of the first century. John did not plot out world history. Rather, he spoke about people and events the first readers could easily identify. As with all apocalyptic, he had to do this in veiled language, but within the tradition of this genre, its references were clear enough. If Revelation was to be helpful to its recipients, it had to speak to their time. It would do little to bolster their endurance to tell them that they should remain faithful and hopeful in these difficult times because God would act decisively on their behalf—in about 2,000 years! As with all apocalyptic writers, John assures the readers that God will act soon (1:1; 6:9–11; 22:20). Thus, Revelation can never be used to predict when the end will come because it envisions only characters and events of the first century.

That Revelation cannot be used to plot out history is also clear from the ways that it moves in cyclical patterns. It does not produce a chronological sequence of events that lead to the end. Instead, it often describes the consequences of disobeying God, looking at those consequences from different perspectives. The seven seals of chapters 6 and following are a good example. These seals reveal what happens in the areas of politics, war, and economics when people disobey God. The order of these things is not important, but rather that they are all consequences of not living as God would have humans live. If the book of Revelation gave the blueprint for world history, chapter 11 would have concluded it. At the end of chapter 11 the day of judgment has arrived and "The kingdom of the world has become the kingdom of the Lord and of his Messiah" (v. 15). This concludes all of world history, the victory of God is secured, the righteous are rewarded, and the wicked are punished (vv. 16–18). But, of course, the book does not end here; chapter 12 begins another cycle within the book. The point here is that Revelation does not intend to do what it is often used to do, that is, predict the course of events in the world so that we can predict the day of the end. The reason we cannot predict world history from Revelation is not that we do not understand it well enough, but that it never intended to enable its readers to make such predictions.

The message of Revelation is something far more important than any delineation of the sequence of events that lead to the end. It is the message that whatever those events are, we can be certain that God will be victorious and that we can be with God if we remain faithful.

Chapter 5

Chapter 5 prepares for the first round of major action in Revelation, which begins in chapter 6. In chapters 1–3 John has described the initial epiphany of Christ and has addressed individually each of the seven churches to which he is writing. Chapters 4 and 5 describe heaven and various things John sees there. In chapter 4 John receives an invitation to come into heaven and gets his first glimpse of the throne of God and the worship that surrounds it. This chapter is powerfully theocentric. This emphasis in chapter 4 allows John to give chapter 5 a more christological focus, though he does not lose sight of God.

After John has described the worship of God in chapter 4, he says in 5:1 that he saw a scroll in the hand of God, a scroll that had writing on the inside and the outside and was sealed with seven seals. In verses 2–4 an angel sends out a proclamation asking who is worthy to open the scroll. But no one is found. All regions are searched: heaven, the earth, and the realms under the earth. This exhausts the cosmological possibilities for people of the ancient world. Nearly all people of this time thought that the cosmos was layered, with a number of fairly discrete realms above the earth and one or more below it. So all of creation is searched to find someone worthy to open or even to read this scroll. When no one is found, John begins to weep. This seems curious since John became aware of the scroll shortly before he begins weeping. Given this reaction, it must contain something he wants to know desperately. Most likely he understands that it contains the destiny of the world and the people in it. This is just the information John and his readers need to know as they try to endure persecution. If this scroll is similar to that found in 1 Enoch 93, it is largely a book of doom and woe for the world. Though it may seem ironic to us, this is good news for those suffering because it means their persecutors are being punished and will no longer be able to inflict pain on them. So John is anxious to know about this future and the fate that awaits the faithful and the wicked.

It may be important to note that the one the angel is seeking is not someone who is able to open the scroll and seals, but someone who is *worthy*. That is, someone who is appropriate to the task, someone who has the characteristics required to reveal and proclaim what the scroll contains, which is no less than God's will and judgment.

In verse 5 one of the elders, one of the classes of beings around the throne of God, comforts John by telling him that one has been found to open the scroll. The language used to introduce this character is messianic; he is the lion of Judah and the root of David. In this way, John reveals that the hope for the messiah is fulfilled in this being, in Christ. This one has conquered and so can open the scroll and its seals. The vocabulary of conquering has already appeared in Revelation several times (e.g., 2:7, 11, 17, 26; 3:5, 12, 21). This is one way John speaks of remaining faithful until the end. In the letters to the churches in chapters 2–3, those who conquer are promised life with God and blessings from God. Now, the one who is worthy to open the scroll is seen as the one who sets the paradigm for the faithfulness of the conquerors who follow him. The conquering this messianic figure accomplishes may be even more specific. Some would argue that since the emphasis of conquering is on faithfulness, the death of Jesus makes him the conqueror. Others assert this must be a reference to the resurrection of Christ because this figure is portrayed as victorious. It seems best not to separate these two parts of the single event of the death and resurrection of Christ. Each gives meaning to the other and they are not understandable if separated to any significant extent. So Christ is seen as conqueror because he was faithful even unto death and then was raised by God. Both the death and the resurrection play a role in the description of him found in the following verses.

When John sees him, this one who is worthy is standing between the throne of God and the four living creatures and among the elders. These beings and the Lamb's location among them are significant. The living creatures are cherubim of some sort. Their presence and description here probably go back to Ezekiel's vision of the four creatures who carry the chariot-throne of God (Ezek. 1:4–14). Their form may draw on Babylonian mythology, which had four winged guardians at the four corners of the earth. In John's revelation, their purpose is to praise God, particularly to lead the heavenly worship by proclaiming God's holiness. With all of their eyes, they probably also represent God's omniscience.

The twenty-four elders are somewhat more difficult to identify and interpreters have suggested several possibilities. Some assert that they represent the ranks of priests in Israel. Others think this image draws on the Roman custom of having presiding officials, including the emperor, surrounded by lesser officials when holding court. This would help make the contrast between emperor worship and worship of the one God even more stark. The image and number may also be related to the twenty-four judges of Babylonian astrology. If they are related to this background they may symbolize cosmic order and governance. The most common understanding of these elders is that they represent the whole people of God by combining the twelve tribes of Israel and the twelve apostles. This understanding may be supported by their possession of bowls full of the prayers of the saints (v. 8). The main activity in which they are engaged in chapters 4 and 5 is worship. Throughout chapter 4 this is directed to God, and in chapter 5 it expands to include the Lamb. Verse 8 tells us that these elders offer incense to God from golden bowls. That this incense represents the prayers of the saints is important because this image gives John's readers reason to take courage and to be hopeful: Their prayers have risen into the direct presence of God.

The messianic figure of verse 4 is identified in verse 6 as a Lamb who had been slaughtered, but who lives and has seven horns and seven eyes. This picture purposefully contains completely incongruous images. The Lamb is probably to be understood as a sacrificial Lamb because it has been killed. But even though it has been killed, it lives. In addition, it has seven horns and seven eyes. Horns were a sign of power and the number seven represents completeness or perfection. So we have a Lamb, that has been killed and yet possesses perfect, complete power. This powerful, yet slain, Lamb also possesses the seven spirits of God. The seven eyes probably indicate that the Lamb sees and knows all and perhaps that he is all wise. The juxtaposition of the symbols of power and weakness is a reminder that the persecution the readers are enduring is not the last word. In fact, God's power is seen even more clearly when viewed in conjunction with the weakness of the Lamb. This Lamb, which was so weak that it was killed, has the full power of God. Perhaps this also explains how the Lamb can also be the lion (v. 5). These oppositions in the description of the Lamb indicate that things are not as they appear on earth; there is a larger reality that is the dominant and lasting reality.[2]

This slain, powerful Lamb is found among the elders. If the elders represent the whole people of God (as most interpreters think), then the Lamb is found among the people of God. This is another bit of encouragement for those suffering persecution, for the risen, powerful Christ is with them in their suffering.

When the Lamb takes the scroll from the hand of God, the living creatures and the elders fall down to worship the Lamb. In the context of Revelation, this worship indicates that the Lamb is accorded the status of divinity. However, there is a very clear distinction between the Lamb and the one seated on the throne, and the Lamb is clearly subordinate. This subordination is seen not only in the position of the Lamb (i.e., not on the throne) but also in the doxological hymn that follows.

John identifies the material in verses 9–10 as "a new song" that the living creatures and the elders sing to the Lamb. The newness of the song indicates that something new has happened for which a new expression of praise is to be sung. This intimates that Christ's death and resurrection (mentioned in verse 9) initiated something new and established Christ as the one who is worthy to reveal and dispatch God's future. This text anchors the salvific work of Christ in an eschatological context.

The hymn asserts that the Lamb is worthy to take the scroll and open it *because* he was slain and purchased a people for God with his blood. So it is the sacrifice of the Lamb for all people that makes him worthy. This hymn may imply that the death and resurrection of Jesus were necessary parts of the echatological scheme, so that God's plan can move ahead once that action has been accomplished. John's assertion that the blood of the Lamb bought a people for God probably draws on the use of this same word in the manumission of slaves who were often symbolically bought by a god "for freedom." Here, these people are purchased for God. In this transaction, the Lamb makes from those of many nations and peoples a single kingdom and priesthood for God. Thus, they are brought together and given a common and esteemed identity and positions of honor and access to God.

The last line of the hymn promises a reality that must have been unimaginable for the original recipients of this book—"they will reign on earth." This promise asserts that there will be a complete reversal of fortunes, it will be a world where the righteous rule. Given the hopeless state of the world described in most of Revelation and apocalyptic literature more broadly, it seems most likely that the earth they will reign on will be the "new earth" spoken of later in the book because the present earth is too corrupt to be redeemed.

Following this hymn, a chorus of tens of thousands of angels join the living creatures and the elders who proclaim "the

Lamb that was slaughtered" worthy of great powers and blessings (vv. 11–12). Then the chorus expands even more to include all creatures in all realms ascribing blessing, honor, and glory to the one on the throne and to the Lamb. This acclamation by such a large company may intentionally call to mind (and surpass) the acclamations of the emperor by many peoples on various occasions. If so, this passage again reflects the conflict John sees between the rule of God and the rule of Caesar. A chorus that includes all created beings can only represent the ultimate victory of God when all beings everywhere recognize God as God. Thus, we have an advance glimpse of the glory of the End.

Interestingly, John has brought the one on the throne back into the picture as these doxologies come to a close. God remains the primary author of all, but the Lamb is praised in ways that are only appropriate for God in Judaism. This close association between the two without identifying them with each other is difficult. John is walking a tightrope. He is trying to maintain monotheism while at the same time honoring Christ as the revelation of God to humanity. John was not the last person to struggle with this matter, but his imagery helped him express the closeness of Christ to God even as he maintained their distinctive identities and positions.

Chapters 4–5 set the stage for the action that begins in chapter 6, when the Lamb begins to open the seals. Chapters 4–5 are a necessary and strengthening element in the flow of Revelation. These chapters offer assurance that the battle in which John's readers are engaged will be won by God. Chapter 5 also makes it clear that the lamb has already achieved the victory, for himself and for all peoples. Thus, their commitment to God is appropriate because the victory of God is assured. As Eugene Boring points out, the doxologies in chapters 4–5 take us from creation to consummation.[3] They show that the God who brought the creation into being will reclaim it in the end. These doxologies celebrate as a reality the victory of God that the readers do not yet experience, but through these hymns they are given the assurance that no other outcome is possible. With this assurance they can face the tribulations in store for them and the whole world, which the following chapters of the book describe. And, of course, these difficulties lead to a fuller description of the victory of God and their participation in it.

Two Sermons on Revelation 5

As noted in the exegetical section, chapters 4 and 5 of Revelation describe heaven and a service of worship taking place there. The emphasis in Revelation 4 is on the enthroned God, who lives forever and ever and, as creator of all, deserves to receive worship from all. In Revelation 5, the Lamb of God enters this gathering. Contrary to what many might expect, the heavenly Lamb still bears the marks of slaughter. This image forces the reader to remember the price that the Lamb has paid for remaining faithful to God. The first sermon that follows, "Worthy Is the Lamb," attempts to deal with our discomfort with the slaughtered Lamb, our embarrassment with the bloody crucifixion and its importance in Christian theology and practice.

The second sermon, "A Good Time to Worship," responds less to the particular content of Revelation 5 than it does to the place chapters 4 and 5 have in the larger narrative. Revelation addresses people who consider themselves oppressed and persecuted. Most of the book describes terrible plagues and destruction that reflect an intense, cosmic struggle and an earthly battle between good and evil. God will win this struggle, but before that ultimate victory many believers will suffer and die. Yet before recounting that vision, the narrator pauses to describe a service of worship. That suggests that just as everything ends with God, so should everything begin with God. Even though beasts, a dragon, and great conflict loom close on the horizon, the narrator still deems that a good time to worship.

"Worthy Is the Lamb"

The events narrated in the fifth chapter of Revelation take place in the throne room of heaven. In the previous chapter, a heavenly worship service begins. In the verses immediately preceding this reading, twenty-four elders bow in homage before God and sing,

You are worthy, our Lord and God,
>   to receive glory and honor and power,
> for you created all things,
>   and by your will they existed and were created.

>   (Rev. 4:11)

Such an ethereal scene and such lofty words of praise make us expect a stunning climax to this service of worship. Perhaps a choir of angels under the direction of Handel, accompanied by Mozart, singing a cantata written by Bach. Perhaps a chorus of cherubs singing the latest praise songs to the rhythm of drums, guitar, and bass. The imagined conclusion of the liturgy will vary according to our individual tastes and preferences, but the picture is clear. This is worship in heaven! This is worship in the immediate presence of God! What could possibly go wrong?

Contrary to our expectations, something can and does go wrong. Instead of having our ears directed toward a musical crescendo, the text directs our eyes to a sealed scroll in the hand of God. Instead of joyful music, a troublesome question rises to our ears: "Who is worthy to open the scroll and break its seals?" (Rev. 5:2). Instead of the sounds of triumph, we hear a weeping prophet lament that no one—no one in heaven—is worthy to open the scroll.

Our anxiety quickly abates, however, at the mention of "the Lion of the tribe of Judah, the Root of David"(5:5). Now that this conquering hero has arrived, surely the service of worship can return to the heights with which it began. But then, as we start to relax, there comes an unexpected description of our hero: "Then I saw between the throne and the four living creatures and among the elders a Lamb standing as if it had been slaughtered" (Rev. 5:6). Slaughtered? The Lamb of God standing in heaven slaughtered? Slaughtered! Both the word and the concept are ugly. But three times in this passage that takes place in the throne room in heaven the Lamb is described as slaughtered. Indeed, the service comes to a climax "with myriads of myriads and thousands of thousands, singing with full voice, 'Worthy is the Lamb that was slaughtered'" (Rev. 5:11–12). Slaughtered? Can't we escape the blood hymns even in heaven? When we draw this close to the throne of God (and the end of the world?), can't we finally put the slaughtered Lamb behind us?

The slaughtered Lamb, the picture of Jesus crucified, is both scandalous and embarrassing. It stretches the imagination to think of God becoming incarnate, of flesh housing divinity. But that paradox alone will not suffice for Christianity. After conceiving of God taking flesh, we slaughter that flesh on a cross and watch God die. Why? Why must Christianity be so bloody? Why not be content with a Jesus who teaches lessons more profound than any heard before or since? Why not be satisfied with a Jesus who stirs the entire world with the life-changing power of his preaching? Why not settle for a Jesus who performs the most wonderful wonders and the most miraculous miracles that the world has ever seen? Why must Christianity return so adamantly to Golgotha and the cross?

To respond to those and similar questions, we must visit the heart of what Jesus and his ministry represent. Jesus does not represent the model picture of humanity. He does not stand for the heights we can attain or the goodness we can acquire by conducting ourselves well enough or righteous enough. Nor in Jesus do we have the mark by which God wants us to measure ourselves. Jesus says, "Follow me" and "Come to me" and even "Get behind me!" but he never says, "Become what I am." Quite to the contrary, Jesus represents God's decision to allow us to have what we cannot attain, to let us reach what we cannot touch.

If we could solve life's most perplexing problems and eliminate sin from our lives simply by learning how best to respond to life, we would need nothing more than a teacher. But, as many of us discovered in algebra class, knowing the correct equation does not always mean solving the problem. Knowledge won't save us. If we could solve life's most perplexing problems and eliminate sin from our lives simply by focusing on the answers we've been given and staying motivated, we would need nothing more than a preacher. That won't work either. We all have lamented with Paul, "I do not do the good I want, but the evil I do not want is what I do" (Rom. 7:19). Will and desire won't save us either. If we could solve life's most perplexing problems and eliminate sin from our lives simply by remembering those times when the power and presence of God almost overwhelmed us, we would need nothing more than a miracle worker. But we typically forget in Capernaum on the fourth day the origin of the wine we drank in Cana on the third day. Signs and wonders won't save us either. We're far too forgetful for that. In the metaphor of Revelation 5, none of us is worthy to open the scroll. None of us. Not one. Not even if and when we make it to heaven.

That is where the cross and the slaughtered Lamb of God enter the picture. The cross represents God's gracious decision to remain involved in our lives whether or not we know or deserve it. The cross represents God's gracious decision to live in relationship with us even though we do not do the good we want to do but rather the evil we do not want to do. Some of us talk about atonement, satisfaction, expiation, or propitiation. Some of us offer theological explanations and metaphors that make the head spin. But regardless of how we explain or describe it, the cross represents God's eventual and ultimate triumph over both the worst we can do and the worst that can be done to us. The cross stands for God's gracious decision to take us past where we can go alone, to let us reach what we cannot touch.

No, this does not explain all the "whys" and "hows" of the cross. That's not necessary. In matters of life and death, explaining the cross matters far less than believing and accepting it. Sin and evil often loom large, heinous, and utterly inescapable. It can make all the difference in (and out of) the world to believe we are not alone and are not dependent on ourselves alone.

Consider the Christians for whom Revelation was written. They were not wealthy people. Many of them survived from day to day. Unlike believers in days to come, who enjoyed the benefit of having the government look favorably on them, they were considered strange and antisocial. Because of their faith, they refused to worship the god of the city in which they lived. That caused them to be labeled unpatriotic. Because of their faith, they avoided the temples where food and other gifts were distributed. In our world, that would be like refusing to let our children celebrate Thanksgiving. The tongues of the neighbors surely wagged and their fingers pointed. Because of their faith, many Christians would not participate in their trade guilds, since they often were associated with temples to various deities. That made it harder for them to practice their trades and thus to earn a living. As a result, Christians found themselves cut off from their neighbors, estranged from their families, and shunned by society. They could not change those realities for themselves. They could, however, believe that God, who raised Jesus from death when people did the worst they could do to him, could and would remain with them as well. That didn't explain all of their "whys" and "hows," but it let them keep going, confident that by the grace of God they could reach what they could not touch.

Sometimes our experience of evil and our need for God are more personal. Several years ago a parishioner called me in the middle of a beautiful summer Saturday afternoon and asked me to go with her to the home of a friend. The friend's eight-year-old child had just drowned in a pond on their farm. By the time I arrived, the shock had become too much for this grieving mother. When I opened my car door, I could hear her screaming. As I stepped onto the front porch, I could see her frantically jerking and pacing in the child's bedroom. I often think that if my parishioner had not been standing behind me, I would have turned and fled. I entered the door knowing nothing to say. As our eyes met, I said and did nothing, but mysteriously she stopped screaming almost immediately. Then she allowed me to help her to sit down. When her sobbing stopped and she caught her breath enough to speak, I could see a spark of hope flash in her eyes. She was still grieving but she was no longer trembling. Then she looked at me and said: "He knows, doesn't he? God knows. He's lost a son too." Forget the explanations. At that moment they didn't matter. And no, nothing anyone could do or did would replace that eight-year-old boy or completely heal the wound in his mother's heart. She had to deal with her loss; but she did so with hope. A slaughtered Lamb gave her hope. She believed, as she faced this evil every parent dreads, that she was not alone. That made all the difference in the world.

At one point or another, we all encounter an evil too powerful to defeat, a sin too strong to resist, a dream we cannot achieve, a good we want to touch but cannot reach. We run into situations in which someone else must do for us what we cannot do for ourselves. It costs something to hold evil and sin in check. It costs something for dreams to come true. It costs something for us to reach what we cannot touch. In the language of faith, the slaughtered Lamb pays that cost.

I still don't like it. I do not understand the slaughtered Lamb. I tremble when imagining the slaughtered Lamb. My eyes want to refuse to behold the sight of the slaughtered Lamb. But when I confess how much more than what I am I would like to become, when I admit that I cannot travel alone to the most wonderful places I want to go, and when I realize how much good there is beyond my touch that I want to reach, I also whisper, sing, and sometimes even shout, "Worthy is the Lamb that was slaughtered!" (Rev. 5:12). Don't we all?

"A Good Time to Worship"

Several images in Revelation 5 catch the eye of a preacher hungry for a sermon. It would be challenging, for example, to reflect on the differences between the names used for Jesus and the word picture of him drawn in the passage. The elder in verse 5 of the vision refers to Jesus as "the Lion of the tribe of Judah" and "the Root of David." Yet Jesus appears in the very next verse as "a Lamb standing as if it had been slaughtered." In Jesus, the lion and lamb don't just lie down together, they become one! There's a sermon there somewhere.

I also find intriguing the image in verse 8 of "golden bowls full of incense, which are the prayers of the saints." That echoes the petition in Psalm 141:2:

> Let my prayer be counted as incense before you,
>   and the lifting up of my hands as an evening
>   sacrifice.

Does God savor the aroma of our prayers? That, too, provides grist for the sermon mill.

Theological eyebrows rise when the four living creatures and twenty-four elders sing to the Lamb, "by your blood you ransomed for God saints from every tribe and language and people and nation" (Rev. 5:9). Ransom? Isn't that something paid to people who take hostages? Some translations have "redeemed" instead. Redeem? Isn't that something once done with coupons? What does either term have to do with Jesus and his ministry?

As intriguing as those possibilities are, as I studied this text this time something else caught my eye. It wasn't something in the text as much as something about the text. Chapters 4 and 5 of Revelation occupy a special place in the overall narrative. In order to see it, let's back up and look at the forest.

When someone mentions Revelation, what comes to mind? For some people, readings of scripture at funerals have imprinted on their minds the picture of a new heaven and a new earth in Revelation 21. Revelation envisions a time of no more death, no more tears, and no more mourning. For others, the events that precede this new heaven and new earth come to mind: wars in heaven, battles with frightening beasts, plagues, and natural disasters. Both place the emphasis on the end of the world and the events that inaugurate or characterize it.

That emphasis is appropriate. The opening verse identifies this unusual book as "[t]he revelation of Jesus Christ, which God gave him to show his servants what must soon take place" (Rev. 1:1). Six verses later we hear this announcement about Jesus:

> Look! He is coming with the clouds;
>> every eye will see him,
> even those who pierced him;
>> and on his account all the tribes of the earth will
>> wail.
>
> (Rev. 1:7)

The rest of chapter 1 and the following two chapters take a brief side trip with their letters to the churches. When chapter 4 begins, however, John sees a door open in heaven and hears a trumpet-like voice command, "Come up here, and I will show you what must take place after this" (Rev. 4:1). Those things that must take place fill most of the pages of the book. Some of those things are frightening. The four horsemen of the apocalypse ride into chapter 6, carrying warfare, slaughter by the sword, famine, death, and Hades. In chapter 8, trumpet-blowing angels bring destruction to one third of the earth, the sea, the sun, the moon, and the stars. In the next chapter, one third of humankind dies. The picture is clear. What must soon take place includes many terrifying events.

Between the opening of chapter 4 and all of those terrifying events, however, we find something we may not suspect. Chapters 4 and 5 make no mention of destruction or suffering. Instead, they describe a service of worship–not just any service of worship, but a service of worship in heaven before the throne of God.

First, John sees God sitting on the throne, receiving worship from a variety of heavenly creatures, who sing without ceasing:

> Holy, holy, holy,
> the Lord God the Almighty,
> who was and is and is to come. (Rev. 4:8)

Then twenty-four elders, who probably symbolize the twelve patriarchs of the Old Testament and the twelve apostles of the New Testament (and thus both covenantal peoples), bow before God and add their song to the liturgy:

> You are worthy, our Lord and God,
>   to receive glory and honor and power,
> for you created all things,
>   and by your will they existed and were created.
>   (Rev. 4:11)

Then chapter 5 begins and we hear about the scroll in God's right hand. But before the scroll is opened our gaze is directed to the Lamb, and as soon as he appears the heavenly creatures and the twenty-four elders join their voices in another song that extols the Lamb. (There surely is a lot of singing in heaven, isn't there?) The intensity of the service increases as angels numbering "myriads of myriads and thousands of thousands" (Rev. 5:11) lend their voices to yet another song of praise:

> Worthy is the Lamb that was slaughtered
> to receive power and wealth and wisdom and might
> and honor and glory and blessing! (Rev. 5:12)

Finally the service comes to a stirring climax and crescendo: "Then I heard every creature in heaven and on earth and under the earth and in the sea, and all that is in them, singing, 'To the one seated on the throne and to the Lamb be blessing and honor and glory and might forever and ever!'" (Rev. 5:13).

Again the picture is clear. John sees a vision of an exuberant, lively, and reverent service of worship. Nothing can deter this service of worship. The scroll, as John's audience and those familiar with such literature know, probably will say something about the destiny of the world, but it remains unopened in the hand of God. Before it is opened, even if that means a delay in "what must soon take place," all creatures come together to worship God.

Isn't that just a little curious? The entire book is about "what must soon take place" and the scroll in the hand of God almost certainly will reveal that, yet everything stops for a service of worship. Why? Why interrupt the narration of "what must soon take place" with a service of worship?

That "why" becomes more emphatic when we think about the people to and for whom John wrote. For Christians, the end of the first century was not the best of times. Although most scholars no longer identify the reign of the Roman emperor Domitian as a time of empire-wide persecution of Christians, there were places where the well-being and lives of Christians were threatened simply because of their faith. That seems foreign to those of us living in the United States, but Christians in places such as India and China will understand very well. The state does not have to support or enforce persecution of a minority for it to occur and possibly thrive.

But overt persecution was not the only problem first-century Christians faced. The local sandalmakers, carpenters, and rug weavers held their union meetings in assembly halls attached to temples and often ate food that had been offered in sacrifice to the gods of those temples. Many Christians felt that they could not participate in those gatherings. That deprived them of the benefits of collegiality with others in their vocation, particularly the lower prices gained from purchasing materials together in bulk. Since most people lived day to day, that meant less money in the pocket and less food on the table. It also meant that they made themselves identifiably different, and we all know what happens when people isolate themselves for religious reasons. Just think how we treat the "fanatics" who refuse to go along with social norms because of their faith.

Many first-century Christians also refused to make sacrifices "to the health of the emperor" because they considered that to be paying homage to the emperor as a god. That caused others to consider them unpatriotic. It also meant that Christians did not receive the gifts often distributed by the government at temple gatherings, often a gift of meat or other food. Imagine knowing that your children went to bed hungry because you were a Christian. Imagine what the neighbors would think of you.

Once again, the picture is clear. Being a Christian in the first century meant depriving oneself of social and economic advantages, facing occasional harassment or persecution, and running the considerable risk of angering Rome or the local powers that be. There was nothing easy about that. Surely the early Christians wanted to know how John's vision would help them to deal with the difficulties they faced. That brings us back to our questions. Why? Why interrupt the narration of "what must soon take place" with a service of worship?

To a people who may be wondering whether the price they are paying for being Christian is too high, John seems to say as loudly and clearly as possible, "God always deserves worship." Yes, the times were hard. Yes, Christians were misunderstood and mistreated. But that changed nothing. God deserved worship at all times. As a matter of fact, in heaven, where things are as they should be, God receives worship "day and night without ceasing" (Rev. 4:8). No matter what happens in our world or the world, God deserves worship.

John believed that. Do we? Do we consider worship not merely something good to do but something essential, something necessary? Do we believe that nothing that has taken place or soon will take place in our lives should interfere with our worship of God? At the risk of going from preaching to meddling, I think not. The discrepancy between our membership roll and the average attendance at services of worship suggests not. Do all or even most of the people who claim to be Christian worship God on a regular basis? I think not.

I hear the murmurs. "Preacher, you've crossed the line. Things were different then than they are now."

That's right. Things were different. It's a lot easier now! Unlike the Roman Empire during the first century or India or China during the twentieth century, when we gather for worship no one will taunt us, hurl abuse at us, or threaten our lives. Unlike the Roman Empire during the first century or India or China during the twentieth century, we will not suffer financially or be ostracized socially for gathering to worship God. When we compare our situation with theirs, we realize that we have nothing to lose and they have a lot to lose, possibly even their lives.

"But, preacher," the murmur continues, "you sound too legalistic. We're saved by grace, not by perfect worship attendance!" That's true; but is worship entirely optional? Is it an elective in the curriculum of Christianity or a requirement? Is there ever a time when God does not deserve worship?

"Let's be reasonable, preacher. Although all of us have excuses rather than reasons for most of the times we fail to worship, our absences aren't always simply a matter of convenience. Sometimes it hurts to come to worship. Sometimes gathering to worship only exacerbates an already difficult situation."

All of us know about those times, or we will soon enough.

For thirty years you worship together, she on the front row of the choir loft and you on the third pew from the back on the right. Then a heart attack claims her. When Sunday comes, even the thought of sitting in that pew without seeing her in the choir brings you to tears. Is that a good time to worship?

You made a mistake, a stupid mistake. The local newspaper chose to make that mistake front page news. How can you face your friends in the congregation? How many more times can you tell the story and express your remorse? Each familiar face only deepens the pain and the shame. It doesn't even help to be told that they still care about you. Actually, at the moment that kindness feels like a curse. Is that a good time to worship?

You've never thought of yourself as a public speaker, but you decide to address the school board because your heart won't let your tongue stay still. The position you advocate isn't popular, but you have prayed about it, talked with your friends about it, and spoken to your pastor about it. You don't know how a Christian can do or think anything else. Your words do not settle easily on the ears of your neighbors. They are, however, far gentler than the words shouted at you in reply. You acted with conviction, admitting that you could be wrong but declaring with all your heart that you thought you were right. No one stood behind you. No one. Not all of them spoke against you, but none of them rose to support you. None of them. How could you possibly sing "Blest Be the Tie that Binds" on Sunday when you have never felt so alone on Thursday? Is that a good time to worship?

Such influences and situations may not sound like the four horsemen of the apocalypse, but they certainly feel like warfare, slaughter, famine, death, and Hades. Surely God doesn't expect us to worship under such conditions. How could we? What good would it do?

God doesn't have a scorecard on which to mark all the times we skip a service of worship. Nor does the heavenly host include liturgical police on the prowl for truant Christians. Nor will we fall from grace if we miss two or more consecutive services of worship. Yet, even in the situations described and worse—like those of first-century Rome and many places in twentieth-century India and China—it is a good time to worship.

The situations sketched earlier describe times that test our faith, times when believing does not come easily. Those are hard times, demanding times, times that ask more of us than any other. Whom do we need more than God to get through such times? If we're angry and want to demand, "Why, God?" the God we worship can take it. Read the book of Psalms. God has had a lot of practice dealing with angry people trying to continue to believe. Are we broken and feeling utterly abandoned? Who better than God to heal and shepherd us? Even the worst of times are good times to worship.

There is some unexpected grace that comes with this. I have a colleague who insists that sometimes we come to worship so that others can worship for us.[4] When we lack the will to sing "Amazing Grace," we come to worship so that others can give voice to what we want to believe and receive. When it hurts even to think of coming to God in prayer, we come to worship so that others can pray not only for us but also in our place. When we cannot see past the mountain of hurt and the twisted road of disappointment that separates us from God, we come to worship so that God can use others to make the rough places plain and the crooked straight. When we need someone else to speak to God, sing to God, and believe in God because we're not sure we can, that is a good time to worship.

The next time we have not a reason but an excuse for missing worship we can remember that. Someone about whom we care may need our voice that day. That, too, makes it a good time to worship.

Please do not interpret this as a legalistic requirement. Please do hear this as a fervent exhortation to recognize the necessity of worship for our well-being as congregations and as individuals. God deserves worship and we need to worship. In worship we remember that we have somewhere and someone other than ourselves to whom to turn. In worship we hear whispers of the God who seems absent and silent. In worship we receive gifts of bread and cup that have nothing to do with what we deserve and everything to do with what we need. In worship we find at least a few moments of sanctuary from the world that often seems too much with us. That makes any time a good time to worship.

> Then I heard every creature in heaven and on earth and under the earth and in the sea, and all that is in them, singing,
>
> "To the one seated on the throne and to the Lamb, be blessing and honor and glory and might for ever and ever!"

> And the four living creatures said, "Amen!" And the elders fell down and worshiped. (Rev. 5:13–14)

Whatever was going on in John's life when he had that vision and whatever is going on in our lives now, all creation seems to consider it a good time to worship. Do we?

By the grace of God, may it be so. By the grace of God, so it is!

CHAPTER 8

Revelation 14

Exegesis

The first half of Revelation concludes with the end of chapter 11, where the kingdom of God is established and the day of judgment has come. Instead of ending there, John begins a new set of visions, visions that cover the same period of time as the previous larger cycle but provide a different viewpoint on some things and encourage faithfulness among his readers.[1] The new start at chapter 12 begins with a "great sign," and chapter 14 concludes the first cycle of visions in this second major section of visions. While the details of the visions in chapters 12–13 are sometimes obscure and difficult, it seems clear by the end of chapter 13 that the primary evil being characterized is the emperor cult. Inhabitants of many cities were required to offer incense to the genius of the emperor at this time. Deification of the emperor had developed to the point that Domitian was even requiring people to address him as "our lord and god."

Chapter 13 concludes by speaking of the emperor cult as the beast whose number is 666, a number that is further identified as a "human number" (v. 18). Calling it a "human number" means that it represents someone's name. Using numerology (assigning letters of the alphabet a numerical value—a well-known practice in the ancient Mediterranean world), the identity of this person is intended to be fairly easy for John's readers to discern. Most critical interpreters agree that the person referred to with this number is Nero. But even that name is symbolic, representing the emperor, because Nero was probably already dead when Revelation was written. So it is the emperor and the emperor cult that are identified as the enemy of the people of God at the end of chapter 13.

Chapter 14 begins with a break in the action that has been constant and violent since the beginning of chapter 12. Such breaks are common in Revelation. Chapter 14:1–5 provides a glimpse into heaven and of the Lamb on Mount Zion. With the Lamb are 144,000 who have on their foreheads the names of the Lamb and of God. This seal indicates that they have been faithful to God (see Ezek. 9) and that they now belong to God as God's own possession. Their identity as God's own possession is reinforced by John's saying that they have been bought (redeemed) from among humanity to be God's and the Lamb's (v. 4). The number 144,000 is symbolic. It is derived from two complete numbers, 12 and 10 (12x12x10x10–in chapter 7, there are 12,000 from each of the twelve tribes). Twelve was, of course, also the number of tribes in Israel. Thus, it symbolizes the complete number of this group. These 144,000 are the antithesis of those who have the mark of the beast (13:16–17). John identifies them as the firstfruits for God and the Lamb and those who follow the Lamb wherever he goes. These characteristics probably indicate that the 144,000 are martyrs because they are willing to follow the Lamb even to death and are the first sample of the whole people of God, who are now being encouraged to remain faithful as they see the position that previous martyrs occupy. As the firstfruits they are also a pledge that the rest of the harvest will be successful. Having 144,000 in this group implies that the full number of martyrs must be completed before the end comes, and it implies that these faithful ones will be victorious.

Those in this group are also said to have not "defiled themselves with women," to be free from lying, and to be blameless. The first of these characteristics may indicate that John valued lifelong celibacy and thus advocated a somewhat ascetic ideal. While this possibility is more probable than is usually acknowledged, the sexual purity mentioned here may be metaphorical. Adultery is nearly always symbolic in Revelation: It stands for idolatry. John probably took this metaphor from the prophets of the Hebrew Bible, who often used it to speak of Israel's going after other gods. If this metaphorical interpretation is correct, then the contrast between these faithful 144,000 and those sealed with the mark of the beast is yet more emphatic. Furthermore, it may be that the lie that is not found in their mouths is that of denying their faith in face of persecution.

These 144,000 are probably also the ones who are singing the "new song" before God. Though John does not reveal the content of this song, we should probably view it as a song of praise and victory similar to those seen elsewhere in Revelation, perhaps even drawing on the songs of victory the Israelites sang on the other side of the sea after God saved them from the Egyptians (Ex. 15:1–21).

The vision of the joyous, victorious martyrs worshiping before God leads to a vision of a sequence of angels, each of whom proclaim the arrival of the judgment of God (vv. 6ff.). This message of the arrival of God's judgment is called gospel in verse 6. The long-awaited expression of the justice of God is good news for John and his readers. Though this seems strange to us, God's justice is essential if we are going to be able to trust God. God must do what is right and just because God must remain faithful to God's own character. The good news of the justice of God includes judgment in which God punishes evil and rewards righteousness. This first message of good news may also allow for repentance, since the hearers are called to fear God and to worship God.

The second angel proclaims the fall of Babylon (that is, Rome), which will be described in more detail later in chapters 17–18. The third angel specifies the criteria for judgment: participation in the emperor cult and perhaps in other aspects of the pagan culture that John thinks are inappropriate for people who profess faith in God. This angel also describes the punishment of those who engage in the condemned activities. The point of this is not only to see the Christians' enemies suffer, but also to call the readers to faithfulness when they see what happens to those without faith. This point is made explicitly in the immediately following sentence, "Here is a call for the endurance of the saints" (v. 12). Why this announcement of judgment and description of the punishment of the wicked can encourage faithfulness is further explained in verse 13, where John is told to write that those who die in the Lord are blessed, to which the Spirit adds that they will rest from their labors. This, then, is the other side of the judgment—the blessing of the faithful.

Verses 14–20 contain another description of God's judgment on the wicked. In verse 14 John sees one who is "like the Son of Man" seated on a cloud with a crown on his head and a sickle in his hand. "Son of Man" is, of course, the title Jesus usually uses for himself in the Synoptic Gospels. Coming from Daniel 7, this description of a heavenly figure seems related to eschatological expectations but remains vague. While it is possible that "one like the Son of Man" designates Christ as the one on the cloud, verse 15 mentions "another angel" and so seems to identify the "one like a son of man" as an angel.[2] More evidence against identifying this figure with Christ is that yet another angel appears in verse 17 with a sickle and performs the same task as the one on the cloud a second time.

The image of reaping with a sickle to signify God's judgment comes from Joel 3:11–16 (especially v. 13), where Joel summons to the valley of decision the nations that surround and trouble Israel. There they are to be reaped and tread on in the winepress, which overflows with their wickedness. John expands this image to worldwide proportions, a move nearly made by Joel, who spoke of the sun and moon being darkened and the stars retreating at the judgment of God. John's expansion of this image has God's judgment exercised on the whole world rather than having God's judgment of a part of the world produce cosmic repercussions. Since this imagery of reaping is associated with condemnatory judgment in Joel, the two reapings in Revelation 14:14–20 probably both refer to a reaping of the wicked, even though it seems repetitious. Perhaps the first reaping is an initial judgment of God, similar to those in the first half of the book, which were intended in part to lead to repentance (e.g., 9:20–21), followed by the final judgment.

After the reapings are completed, what these beings have reaped is put into the "winepress of the wrath of God." In addition to drawing on Joel 3, John may also echo Isaiah 63:1–6, where God as warrior returns from crushing Edom (a symbol of the enemies of God's people) under his feet in the winepress. The divine warrior in the Isaiah passage says that he alone defeated Edom and that it was his wrath that sustained him in the battle. So the imagery is not new, nor is the idea that God's wrath has a part in judgment. However, God's wrath should not be understood as unbridled anger that outstrips what is appropriate. Rather, God's wrath is the just, fair reaction of a righteous God who has seen the creation abused and God's own people injured. What God's wrath delivers is just punishment, the actions that must be meted out if God is to be a God of justice, power, and love. Such judgment is not optional and it is not cruelty. Without judgment, which includes both condemnation and blessing, God cannot remain God, cannot remain true to God's self. Without just judgment, God cannot be trusted or worshiped. Thus, this punishment of the wicked is a divine necessity, a necessity for which we, with John, should be grateful.

Still, the description of this judgment is gruesome, with blood flowing as deep as a horse's bridle for two hundred miles. This terrible sight intends to show the magnitude of the wickedness God is punishing and the thoroughness of God's justice at the end. The horrific impression this passage makes on us may well have been experienced differently by John's original readers. They knew the pain of persecution, whether it was social and economic alone or whether it included physical violence. Their oppression called for a powerful response from God that proclaimed God understood the depths of their suffering and would not allow such injustice to be the final word. It is important to notice here that this battle against the wicked at judgment is carried out by God alone. The saints will not be loosed to do vengeance with injustice. No! This is a word about the justice and power of God, the God who hates oppression and injustice and the suffering of the righteous. This is also a word about the love God has for God's people: God will enter into judgment to make things just for them. So the purpose of this judgment is to make things fair for the righteous and the wicked and to allow God to remain the God who is worthy of praise and worship. As difficult a passage as this is to hear, "Here is a call for the endurance of the saints."

Chapter 14 is another good example of the cyclical nature of the visions of Revelation. Once the judgment has been accomplished at the end of this chapter, a new series of actions begins: another portent and seven bowls. These bowls expand the compressed actions seen in chapter 14 and will lead to the final descriptions of God's judgment and the establishment of the kingdom of God. One emphasis of the cycle composed of chapters 12–14 is endurance of persecution. In 13:10 and 14:12 John writes that these visions are a call to endurance. These are the only two uses of this word (*hupomonē*) in Revelation after the letters to the seven churches (chapters 2–3). So these initial proclamations of the second large vision cycle of Revelation (chapters 12–21) make explicit that the point of John's visions of God's judgment and of the blessed end of the faithful is to encourage the readers to maintain their faith in the midst of persecution, knowing that the God to whom they are being faithful can and will act in accordance with the character of God—with love, power, and justice.

Two Sermons on Revelation 14

The sermons on Revelation 14 attempt to deal with two topics shunned by many preachers. Funeral services and choral requiems have made most of us very familiar with the words "Blessed are the dead who from now on die in the Lord…[for] they will rest from their labors" (Rev. 14:13). The promise of eternal life always has been and continues to be held dear by faithful Christians. Yet I have no memory of a sermon on the topic and have found colleagues loathe even to mention it in the same sentence with the word *sermon.* "A Good Word for Eternal Life" tries to suggest that even we sophisticated, modern Christians need not feel embarrassed by hoping to live and love beyond our earthly lives and loves.

The final sermon in this collection takes a look at the closing verses of this chapter and attempts to handle a topic that makes us even more uncomfortable. While we may refer to longings for eternal life as "pie in the sky," we have nothing at all to say about the wrath of God. We know that the phrase appears often in the Bible, but at that point most of us become Marcionite and declare that topic outside our canon. "The Wrath of God" attempts to shatter that silence for this preacher, as it strives to examine this topic from the perspective of Revelation and from the viewpoint of a thoroughly modern Christian who still finds the issue of theodicy demanding, yet worthy of being addressed in the pulpit.

"A Good Word for Eternal Life"

All the coins and currency in my pocket have on them the phrase "In God We Trust." I don't remember ever taking note of that when making a purchase. When I pay the bill and pocket the change, I pay close attention to the value of the money but give little mind to the words stamped or printed on it. I do try to make sure that the clerk does not hand me a foreign coin. That, however, has nothing to do with any phrase included or omitted on it. I'm not sure what foreign coins have stamped on them, but I am sure that vending machines won't accept them. Beyond that, it doesn't matter. If the bill or coin will spend, I'll spend it.

I wonder whether I would pay that little attention if the coins and currency had on them phrases such as "In Bill Clinton I Trust" or "Glory Be to George Bush." Would I give it no mind if I found "God of America" stamped above Washington's head on a quarter instead of "Liberty"? Would I feel comfortable handling a twenty-dollar bill that depicted Andrew Jackson sitting on a throne in the clouds? Would I resent tacitly paying homage to a politician every time I made a purchase? Would I find it offensive and refuse to use coins and currency that glorify or deify human beings?

The Christians addressed by Revelation faced a dilemma far worse than that one. By the time Revelation was written, most of the imperial coins, the ones necessary for buying and selling throughout the Roman Empire, bore the image of the emperor depicted as an enthroned deity. Coins authorized by the Emperor Domitian included along with his image the inscription "to Zeus the Supreme, the Savior, the Emperor

Domitian." Beginning with Julius Caesar, the Senate often deified emperors after their death. But by the time of Revelation, living emperors had begun to consider themselves divine and to order their servants to address them as Lord and God. Nearly every major city in the Empire erected a temple, shrine, altar, or statue that promoted emperor worship. Those who refused to sacrifice to the "genius" or health of the emperor were guilty of atheism, not worshiping a deity of the Empire, and treason, taking the side of Rome's enemies by refusing to pray for Rome's leader.

Early Christians considered it blasphemy and idol worship to engage in such "normal" activities as sacrificing to the emperor, worshiping the emperor, participating in public events in which people paid homage to the emperor as to a god, and using money stamped with the emperor's image. They, like the author of Revelation, referred to the emperor as a beast and to anything with the image of the emperor on it as bearing the mark of the beast. Needless to say, that made it almost impossible for Christians to engage in day-to-day commerce, and it made them far from popular with the local authorities charged with enforcing the emperor's decrees. At the least, Christians were considered odd misfits who refused to conform to societal norms. At the worst, they were considered traitors capable of treason. Their neighbors treated Christians just like we treat people that do not fit. Most despised and shunned them. Some humiliated or persecuted them.

Revelation was written to offer encouragement to these Christians. Revelation 14 presents a vision of heaven that assures Christians that God will triumph over those that despise, shun, and persecute them. The seer draws a contrast between the wicked, who worship the emperor and bear the mark of the beast, and the faithful, who bear the mark of the Lamb of God and sing a new song before God. The seer labels the emperor worshipers as defiled and praises the faithful, who keep themselves pure by worshiping God alone. This vision does not make light of the circumstances in which the Christians live. An angel announces, "Babylon [i.e., Rome]... has made all nations drink of the wine of the wrath of her fornication"

(Rev. 14:8). But the vision does include a stirring promise to the faithful. To those who endure persecution without losing faith, a voice from heaven declares, "Blessed are the dead who from now on die in the Lord," and the Spirit adds, "They will rest from their labors, for their deeds follow them" (Rev. 14:13). The faithful may lose their lives, but the gracious Lamb of God will bless them eternally. Their deeds of faith in an evil world will follow them to the throne room of heaven, where at last they will find rest. This blessed state of the persevering faithful stands in stark contrast with the earlier declaration that "There is no rest day or night for those who worship the beast and its image and for anyone who receives the mark of its name" (Rev. 14:11).

Those words probably meant a great deal to the early Christians. With nearly the entire world weighing heavily against them, it must have felt good to have a respected leader insist that God not only took note of them but also promised them rest that does not end. Those words probably meant a great deal to early Christians. What about us?

At a monthly gathering of a local ministerial association, the topic, as usual, turned to preaching. Pastors representing several traditions started to compare their texts and topics for the coming Sunday. One pastor announced that he had known what his topic would be for quite some time. He said that on the Sunday before Memorial Day, he always preached on eternal life. One of his colleagues shook his head and declared, "I could never do that." When asked why, he responded, "What is there to say?"

Before we start asking for the name, address, and denomination of that preacher, let's ask ourselves what we have had to say about eternal life lately. If we haven't attended a funeral, have we heard it mentioned at all? Have we talked about it while relaxing with our friends, during a casual moment at work, or even in church school lately? Although we may not have been as blunt (or as honest) as that preacher, have we had anything to say about eternal life?

In our defense, all of us want to avoid reducing Christianity to "pie in the sky." We have known those who seemed to ignore their neighbors while waiting for the roll to be called up yonder. We have experienced people that triumphantly sing, "Some glad morning, when this life is o'er, I'll fly away," but never quite learn the melody of "They'll Know We Are Christians by Our Love." Christian faith makes claims and issues calls on our lives here and now. But does that leave us bereft of something to say about eternal life? Are we so busy focusing on this time and place that we pay no mind to eternity? Or does our silence reflect something deeper than that?

As we have become more scientific and sophisticated in our thinking, has the notion of eternal life started to embarrass us? As we have learned to place more and more trust in things we can see and prove, have we become less and less accepting of something beyond sight and proof? Have we grown so comfortable with this world that we no longer look or long for another one?

Several years ago, in a youth meeting on the topic of death and dying, a physician stunned me when he told the group: "When you're dead, that's it. You're just dead. There's no pain. There's nothing to fear. You just aren't anymore. You're dead." As the young people asked him questions, it became crystal clear that he meant precisely that and absolutely nothing more. Despite the fact that he participated faithfully in and was a leader of his congregation, he believed that life, all life, any and every kind of life, ended with death. He had nothing to say about eternal life.

Is there nothing to say? Do we eventually reach a point when even God has no power to continue our lives? Do we ultimately come to a truly dead end? Without trying to describe or explain it, do we believe in life beyond this life? Do we have anything to say about eternal life?

The author of Revelation and the people to whom the book first spoke had something to say. They knew that the power of Rome stood behind the policies that called for worship of the emperor, but they believed that only the God "who made heaven and earth, the sea and the springs of water" (Rev. 14:7) deserved worship. They knew that the society in which they lived made little room for and had little patience with people like them, but that did not stifle their belief in "an eternal gospel...to every nation and tribe and language and people" (Rev. 14:6). They knew only too well the difficulties of remaining faithful, the challenges of being recognizably different, the weariness that comes from persevering when persecuted, but that did not diminish their confidence in the promise that "they [would] rest from their labors, for their deeds [would] follow them" (Rev. 14:13). They had no reason to doubt the reality of Rome. They chose to believe just as strongly in a far greater reality they could neither see nor prove. That wasn't "pie in the sky." It was absolute confidence and trust in God.

It takes little effort to discern the power of evil. Simply glance at the newspaper or overhear the evening news. It takes little effort to discover the fragility of human life. Disease, accident, and time's passing illustrate that daily. We have no proof of anything else. We do, however, have a promise: "Blessed are the dead who...die in the Lord...they will rest from their labors, for their deeds follow them" (Rev. 14:13). Believing that promise changes the world. It changes the world from a place tied to our limits to a place touched by the limitless potential of God.

On the eve of his assassination, Dr. Martin Luther King, Jr., delivered a sermon in Memphis, Tennessee. At the beginning of that sermon, he said that he would rather be alive then and there than at any other time in history. He explained that he felt that way not because the path he was following was easy or painless, but because he was convinced that God was at work in the world and in the struggle for civil rights. He concluded that sermon with these words:

> Well, I don't know what will happen now. We've got some difficult days ahead. But it doesn't matter with me now. Because I've been to the mountaintop. And I don't mind. Like anybody, I would like to live a long life. Longevity has its place. But I'm not concerned about that now. I just want to do God's will. And He's allowed me to go up to the mountain. And I've looked over. And I've seen the promised land. I may not get there with you. But I want you to know tonight, that

we, as a people will get to the promised land. And I'm
happy, tonight. I'm not worried about anything. I'm
not fearing any man. Mine eyes have seen the glory of
the coming of the Lord.[3]

Faith wasn't "pie in the sky" for Martin Luther King, Jr. He
knew very well the sting of persecution and the weariness of a
long struggle. But King still had a good word for eternal life, a
word that allowed both him and his followers to persevere regardless of what happened.

On a lazy summer afternoon, I sat beside the deathbed of
a saint we all called Miss Georgia. Miss Georgia had no children of her own, but nearly every child in town knew her and
experienced her love. Even when she no longer could leave
her home, she managed to keep up with what was happening
in the youth groups. Most of the youth didn't know it, but they
never took a trip or completed a project to which she did not
contribute. Miss Georgia knew that death was near that afternoon, but she was absolutely calm. When asked if she had any
fear of dying, she replied: "Of course not. I'm going to live
forever with my children."

"Pie in the sky"? Absolutely not. But a good word for eternal life, a word that brought rest from the labors of a life of
faith.

Eternal life. It isn't a conundrum to solve or a theory to
prove. If it were, it would have nothing to offer us. Our minds
and our understanding cannot stretch that far. But our souls
and our faith can. We can firmly believe that our limits do not
limit what God can do. We can steadfastly believe that when
we have finished living and loving as best we can, God provides a way for living and loving to continue. Girded by such
confidence in God, we can answer the call to "hold fast to the
faith of Jesus" (Rev. 14:12). That doesn't make the life of faith
easy, but it surely is a good word for eternal life.

"The Wrath of God"

The closing verses of Revelation 14 have made Christians
throughout the ages cringe and shudder. They draw a picture
of sickle-swinging angels "harvesting" the wicked, just as farmers

harvest their grapes when they are ripe and throw them into the winepress. The image of a winepress as a metaphor for the judgment of God appeared in Isaiah and Lamentations long before the writing of Revelation,[4] but John's gruesome application of the metaphor makes theirs pale in comparison. In John's vision,

> The angel swung his sickle over the earth and gathered the vintage of the earth, and he threw it into the great wine press of the wrath of God. And the wine press was trodden outside the city, and blood flowed from the wine press, as high as a horse's bridle, for a distance of about two hundred miles. (Rev. 14:19–20)

Among the many ghastly and gory pictures drawn in Revelation, that may be the most offensive.

Many have argued that the God depicted here could not possibly be the God of John 3:16 and Psalm 23. What does this God of wrath have to do with a God who loves the world and cares for the people of faith like a good shepherd? This must be a false picture of God, a picture drawn by someone unbalanced and decidedly unchristian. What kind of twisted mind could create such an image?

Without doubt, this picture of a wrathful God is gruesome, but it does not stand alone in the Bible. Of the many possible examples, let's look at four from four different sections of scripture. In Isaiah, God laments the corruption of Jerusalem and promises to pour wrath on it:

> Your princes are rebels and companions of thieves.
> Everyone loves a bribe and runs after gifts.
> They do not defend the orphan,
>> and the widow's cause does not come before them.
>
> Therefore says the Sovereign, the LORD of hosts, the
>> Mighty One of Israel:
> Ah, I will pour out my wrath on my enemies,
>> and avenge myself on my foes!
>
> (Isa. 1:23–24)

In the book of Psalms, the king of Israel receives a promise that brings a curse on his enemies:

> The Lord is at your right hand;
>> the Lord will shatter kings on the day of divine
>> wrath.
>
> The Lord will execute judgment among the nations,
>> filling them with corpses;
>> the Lord will shatter heads
>> over the wide earth.
>
> (Ps. 110:5–6)

Another mention of God's wrath comes from a familiar voice. We remember that John the Baptizer prepared the way of the Lord, but we sometimes forget this part of his message: "You brood of vipers! Who warned you to flee from the wrath to come?" (Lk. 3:7). We complete our brief tour of divine wrath with a stop in Ephesians. After calling the faithful to renounce fornication, greed, and "obscene, silly, and vulgar talk" (Eph. 5:4), the author warns, "Let no one deceive you with empty words, for because of these things the wrath of God comes on those who are disobedient" (Eph. 5:6). That pretty much includes all of us!

The scene in Revelation 14 makes us cringe, but it has ample biblical company. The wrath of God appears in the Old Testament and the New Testament, in historical, poetic, and prophetic books, in the gospels and the epistles. Whether we like it or not, God's wrath shows up everywhere!

Ubiquitous or not, we don't like it, do we? Most of us deplore this picture of an angry God. What happens, however, if we walk around this elephant and examine it from a different perspective? Do we like the image of God as powerful, powerful enough to protect the powerless? Do we like the image of God as mighty, mighty enough to defeat evil? Do we like the image of God as just, just enough to exonerate the innocent and punish the wicked? Do those images trouble us? Do we like the picture of a God who will stand behind God's word and keep God's promises? Does that trouble us?

In the portion of John's vision narrated in Revelation 13, evil has gotten almost out of hand. John describes evil as a beast with "a mouth uttering haughty and blasphemous words," who makes war on and conquers God's saints and exercises authority over "every tribe and people and language and nation" (Rev. 13:5–7). John considered evil that powerful and threatening. He did so for good reason. He had seen Christians persecuted and even executed because of their faith. He had seen families shunned and abused because as Christians they refused to makes sacrifices to the emperor. He probably had watched Roman legions chase Christians from their homes and slaughter many of them in the streets during the Jewish revolt against Rome. Was it wrong for a person who had seen that and more to have a vision of an angry God? Was it wrong for him to envision a God of justice passing judgment?

We may not have experienced such persecution. I hope that we never will, but some Christians do. Noor Alam, a Presbyterian pastor in Pakistan who built the first Christian church in his area, was rewarded by being stabbed to death in his home in January 1998.[5] Soldiers in Sudan sold a fifteen-year-old Roman Catholic boy into slavery. His owners tied him to a pole, denied him food and water, and beat him with the butt of a gun for twenty-four hours.[6] In November 1998, the United Christian Forum in India complained that in that country, "Nuns have been raped, priests executed, Bibles burnt, churches demolished, educational institutions destroyed and religious personnel harassed." They further charged that acts of violence against Christians had more than doubled between 1964 and 1998.[7] According to an Internet source, Coptic Christians in Egypt complained late in 1998 that kidnapping of Coptic girls by Moslem extremists had become "a weekly routine." A local police chief allegedly told the parents of one kidnapped girl to "forget about her," since there was no hope that she would be found.[8] In those situations and hundreds of others like them, would it be wrong for Christians to conclude that such heinous acts offend God? Could we condemn them for praying for the justice of God or for envisioning God's taking vengeance on those who abuse and violate people of faith?

Perhaps we have not experienced persecution, but we have encountered evils that shake us to the core of our being. The daughter of a friend was raped by someone she knew. He showed no remorse and, in fact, declared that she asked for it. Surely all of us remember the stories of a man tied to the back of a truck and dragged to his death for the "crime" of not being Caucasian and of another man beaten and left hanging on a fence to die because of his sexual orientation. We can add to that stories of bombed and burned churches, various hate crimes, and savage beatings of people who had the misfortune of being in the wrong place at the wrong time. In such situations, don't we all beg with the psalmist, "O God, do not keep silence; do not hold your peace or be still, O God!" (Ps. 83:1)? In such situations, is there anything wrong with longing for the justice of God or with envisioning God's defending the violated and punishing the violator?

John certainly did not consider it wrong to long for and envision the power and justice of God. The image in Revelation that we find so repugnant represents his conviction that God will not keep silent indefinitely, his confidence that at some point God will act, and his belief that God will render just judgment. Even if we do not like the scene he envisions, isn't that good news? When scripture asserts that God will indeed do what is right, that God will protect the powerless, punish evil, and reward faithfulness, isn't that good news?

It is good news when the good take action. I haven't always been this way, but I no longer tremble at the angry roar of those who stand against me. I am not naive about their power, but they don't concern me as they once did. I now find far more threatening the damning silence of those who say they stand with me. They frighten me because I cannot count on their using whatever power they have. John's image, John's decidedly gruesome image, insists that God will take action, that God will not let the power of the wicked remain unchallenged, that God will triumph even where evil seems the most defiant and invincible. That doesn't mean that God isn't gracious. Without God's grace, we all would perish. Rather, it means that God is just. Because we can depend on the justice of our loving God, we can have hope and endure.

Some of us may agree with all of this, but still be where we started. Some of us may believe and hope that God will protect the powerless, punish evil, and reward faithfulness, but still cringe and shudder at John's vision of blood flowing from the winepress of God's wrath as high as a horse's bridle for two hundred miles. We should cringe and shudder. That's the point! No picture of the consequences of ultimate human rejection of God should be pleasant. John probably intended this image, this symbol, this evocative word picture to disturb us. He presents similarly evocative and disturbing word pictures throughout Revelation. Consider, for example, his initial description of Jesus:

> [I]n the midst of the lampstands I saw one like the Son of Man, clothed with a long robe and with a golden sash across his chest. His head and his hair were white as white wool, white as snow; his eyes were like a flame of fire, his feet were like burnished bronze, refined as in a furnace, and his voice was like the sound of many waters. In his right hand he held seven stars, and from his mouth came a sharp, two-edged sword, and his face was like the sun shining with full force. (Rev. 1:13–16)

John reports that when he saw this Jesus he "fell at his feet as though dead" (Rev. 1:17). Who wouldn't? Jesus or not, this is a disturbing picture! Does our discomfort with it, however, make this picture inaccurate or unfaithful? Of course not. Surely we should envision Jesus as powerful, awesome, regal, and mysterious.

We can approach the closing verses of Revelation 14 in a similar fashion. They are disturbing, unsettling, and frightening, but that makes them neither inaccurate nor unfaithful. Don't we believe in and worship a God powerful enough, loving enough, and just enough to protect the innocent, to stand beside the faithful, and to put an end to wickedness and evil? Do we want any less of a God?

As John well knows, we need a disturbingly powerful God. In the chapter preceding the vision of the winepress of God's wrath, John describes evil as a beast, an extremely powerful and frightening beast. He envisions those who worship this beast asking, "Who is like the beast, and who can fight against it?" (Rev. 13:4). John's answer comes in Revelation 14. God can fight against the beast. God can fight against it and God will emerge victorious.

Like John, we know all too well that evil and the evil have power, terrible power, frightening power. They do not, however, have absolute power. Evil and the evil claim dominion over us, but God will reign. Evil and the evil wreak havoc in our lives, but God will execute justice. Evil and the evil taunt us and trample us, but God will not allow that to go unanswered. God will respond. No one should take pleasure in any account of ultimate rejection of God; but all who strive to be faithful can rejoice that those who reject God do not have the final word. God will reward faithfulness and God will protect the faithful. In the first century and on the threshold of the twenty-first century, that's good news! Even if we cringe and shudder as he reports his vision, for this good news we can join our voices with John's and declare, "Thanks be to God!"

Chapter 1: The Problem of Preaching Apocalyptic Texts

[1]Cornish R. Rogers and Joseph R. Jeter, Jr., eds., *Preaching through the Apocalypse: Sermons from Revelation* (St. Louis: Chalice Press, 1992), 1.

[2]Ernst Käsemann, "The Beginnings of Christian Theology," in *New Testament Questions of Today*, trans. W. J. Montague (Philadelphia: Fortress Press, 1969), 102. Cf., in the same volume, "On the Subject of Primitive Christian Apocalyptic," 137.

[3]This comes from the recollection of a conversation between James Mills and Ronald Reagan, who was then governor of California, and is part of an extended conversation quoted in Arthur P. Mendel, *Vision and Violence* (Ann Arbor: University of Michigan Press, 1992), 275–76.

[4]Edward Huenemann, foreword to *Comfort and Protest: The Apocalypse from a South African Perspective*, by Allan Boesak (Philadelphia: Westminster Press, 1987), 9 (author's emphasis).

[5]Hal Lindsey, *The Rapture: Truth or Consequences* (Toronto: Bantam Books, 1983), 10–11.

[6]Quoted in Mendel, *Vision and Violence*, 276.

[7]This phrase belongs to J. Christiaan Beker, *Paul's Apocalyptic Gospel: The Coming Triumph of God* (Philadelphia: Fortress Press, 1982), 27. Beker offers a helpful critique of Lindsey's Bible prophecy on pp. 24–28.

[8]Adela Yarbro Collins, *Cosmology and Eschatology in Jewish and Christian Apocalypticism* (Leiden: E. J. Brill, 1996), 15–16.

[9]Robert R. Wilson, "From Prophecy to Apocalyptic: Reflections on the Shape of Israelite Religion," *Semeia* 21 (1981): 84.

[10]Walter Brueggemann, *Cadences of Home: Preaching among Exiles* (Louisville, Ky.: Westminster John Knox Press, 1997).

[11]Stanley Hauerwas and William H. Willimon, *Resident Aliens: Life in the Christian Colony* (Nashville: Abingdon Press, 1989).

Chapter 2: Apocalyptic Thought

[1]This book is found in the Apocrypha.

[2]Revelation is an exception. It seems to have been written by the person named in the greeting.

[3]This writing is found in the Pseudepigrapha.

[4]This writing is found in the Apocrypha.

[5]The Sadducees are the exception to this trend. They seem not to have believed in an afterlife for anyone. They were also among those who did not adopt an apocalyptic outlook.

[6]This is another work found in the Pseudepigrapha.

[7]This writing is also part of the Pseudepigrapha.

[8]Yet another writing among the Pseudepigrapha.

Chapter 3: Characteristics of an Apocalyptic Preacher

[1]See, for example, Eibert J. C. Tigchelaar, *Prophets of Old and the Day of the End: Zechariah, the Book of Watchers and Apocalyptic* (Leiden: E. J. Brill, 1996), 263–65.

[2]Stephen L. Cook, *Prophecy and Apocalypticism: The Postexilic Social Setting* (Minneapolis: Fortress Press, 1995), 28.

[3]James Melvin Washington, ed., *A Testament of Hope: The Essential Writings of Martin Luther King, Jr.* (San Francisco: Harper and Row Publishers, 1986), 279.

[4]Washington, *Testament of Hope*, 280.

[5]Washington, *Testament of Hope*, 286.

[6]I confess that the Gospel of John has heavily influenced my thinking. The noun *pistis* never appears in the Fourth Gospel, but the verb *pisteúō* appears often.

[7]Beker, *Paul's Apocalyptic Gospel*, 110.

[8]Beker, *Paul's Apocalyptic Gospel*, 16. This is one of six theological issues that Beker derives from Paul's apocalyptic gospel.

[9]David G. Buttrick, *Preaching Jesus Christ: An Exercise in Homiletic Theology*, Fortress Resources for Preaching (Philadelphia: Fortress Press, 1988), 11.

[10]Cf. Käsemann, "On the Subject of Primitive Christian Apocalyptic," 108–111. Käsemann claims that without apocalyptic hope and warning the church would never leave its established positions to take "the necessary step into the freedom of the coming moment at a given point in history" (p. 110).

[11]For a stimulating discussion of Christian accountability, see Leander E. Keck, "The Accountable Self," in *Theology and Ethics in Paul and His Interpreters: Essays in Honor of Victor Paul Furnish*, ed. Eugene H. Lovering, Jr., and Jerry L. Sumney (Nashville: Abingdon Press, 1996), 1–13. For Keck, accountability implies "an acknowledged authority structure in which the self knows that it owes an account and expects a response" (p. 2).

[12]Beker, *Paul's Apocalyptic Gospel*, 86–87, 110.

[13]Quoted in Malcolm Warford, *Our Several Callings: A Foundation Paper on Vocation as a Lifelong Issue for Education* (Bangor, Maine: United Church Board for Homeland Ministries, 1990), 8, who found it quoted in Robert Coles, *Privileged Ones, Volume V of Children of Crisis* (Boston and Toronto: Little, Brown and Company, 1977), 552–53.

[14]For this and the following characteristic of the apocalyptic preacher, I am indebted to Fred B. Craddock, "Preaching the Book of Revelation," *Interpretation* 40 (1986): 270–82. The characteristics reflect Craddock's work, but all culpability for the use of them lies with me.

[15]Do observe that Rev. 5:13 distinguishes the Lamb from the one seated on the throne. Elsewhere, however, the throne appears to belong both to God and to the Lamb (Rev. 7:17; 22:1, 3). In Revelation, as a whole, the picture of who sits on the throne varies. For these pages, let it suffice to conclude that Jesus is enthroned with God.

[16]Fred B. Craddock, "Preaching the Book of Revelation," 275.

[17]This distinguishes traditional apocalyptic thought from that expressed by individuals anticipating a "rapture" that will remove them from the world. Cf. Beker, *Paul's Apocalyptic Gospel*, 27, who criticizes the use of Revelation by Hal Lindsey because it includes "no theology of the cross."

[18]Buttrick, *Preaching Jesus Christ*, 65.

[19]Those who read Greek will notice the intentional pun.

[20]This obedience is a reflection of our relationship with Jesus and not a prerequisite of it. With its insistence on that which God alone can do, apocalyptic thought leaves no room for works-righteousness. We are accountable for responding to the divine purposes, but not responsible for completing those purposes.

[21]Bruce M. Metzger, *Breaking the Code: Understanding the Book of Revelation* (Nashville: Abingdon Press, 1993), 92. This is an excellent resource for Revelation for church groups.

[22]The point for the second half of this message is not that there is nothing we can do, but that victory belongs to God alone. We must respond to what God is doing. That will entail resisting and opposing evil. But we are not responsible for defeating evil. God alone can and will do that.

[23]Cf. Collins, *Cosmology and Eschatology*, 16; and Christopher C. Rowland, "The Book of Revelation: Introduction, Commentary, and Reflections," in *The New Interpreter's Bible. XII. Hebrews, James, 1 and 2 Peter, 1, 2, and 3 John, Jude, Revelation*, ed. Leander E. Keck (Nashville: Abingdon Press, 1998), 506. Collins argues that apocalyptic literature provides new symbolic systems that help us to imagine the social changes needed, and Rowland notes that Revelation "startles, questions, even disorients before pointing to a fresh view of reality."

[24]Cf. L. Susan Bond, "Apocalyptic Vocation and Liberation: The Foolish Church in the World," in *Preaching as a Theological Task: Word, Gospel, Scripture. In Honor of David Buttrick*, ed. Thomas G. Long and Edward Farley (Louisville, Ky.: Westminster John Knox Press, 1996), 150–64. Bond maintains that the eschatological interest of apocalyptic thought provides "the faith community with the confidence to be open to God's future" (154).

[25]Cf. Frederick J. Murphy, "Introduction to Apocalyptic Literature," in *The New Interpreter's Bible. VII. Introduction to Apocalyptic Literature, Daniel, The Twelve Prophets*, ed. Leander E. Keck (Nashville: Abingdon Press, 1996), 3. Murphy maintains that apocalypses "allow the reader to experience the supernatural world that affects this one and to see firsthand the coming eschatological judgment."

[26]This echoes the call for "performative language" issued by many contemporary teachers of homiletics. To those interested in an introduction to the implications of such an approach to preaching, I recommend Walter Brueggemann, "Preaching a Sub-version," *Theology Today* 55 (1998): 195–212. Brueggemann notes that the Hebrew language is imprecise and unclear, making it "a wondrous vehicle for what is suggested but hidden," but annoying to those who think "that if we know the codes, we can pin all meaning down, get all mysteries right and have our own way."

[27]I do not mean to imply that the hearer cannot disagree with the apocalyptic preacher (or any preacher). While the hearer certainly can disagree with the message, the apocalyptic preacher has little or no interest in proving a point and an almost exclusive focus on awakening the hearer to the reality of God and evoking response to that reality. This brings to my mind Ezekiel 3, in which the prophet is told bear witness to what God has revealed to him regardless of whether the people will listen. Similarly, the gospel is not something to prove, but rather something to believe, to accept, and to live.

Chapter 4: Daniel 7

[1]These quotations are taken from the NRSV. The Hebrew word translated as "arrogantly" in verses 8 and 20 of the NRSV is *rabrab*. The Hebrew word translated as "arrogant" in verse 11 is *millah*, which appears again in verse 25, where it is translated as "words." Although the Hebrew words differ, the reality described appears to remain the same.

Chapter 5: 1 Thessalonians 4:13—5:11

[1]*Parousia* is the word often used in the New Testament to refer to the second coming of Christ.

[2]Though some think this may be a word of the risen Christ received by early Christian prophets, it seems much more likely (especially given its parallels with Mt. 24) that Paul knows this as a tradition he has received as a saying of the earthly Jesus.

[3]One might note that this word is a verb, not a noun. Thus, it is used to describe what is happening; the New Testament never calls any event "the Rapture."

[4]Paul uses two negative particles here, two words that mean "no," to make the point emphatic. A reasonable rendering would be, "they will by no means escape."

[5]This armor brings the Thessalonians the Pauline trio of faith, hope, and love, although in a different order.

[6]He has developed this theme in several recent writings. See, for example, Walter Brueggemann, *Cadences of Home: Preaching among Exiles* (Louisville, Ky.: Westminster John Knox Press, 1997).

Chapter 6: Mark 13

[1]This writing is found in the Pseudepigrapha.

[2]For another example of Mark using this device see 5:21–43, where the Gospel writer combines the healing of Jarius' daughter with the healing of the woman with the hemorrhage.

[3]I extend my thanks to the congregation of the Crofton Christian Church, with whom I experienced the events of autumn 1990 and the initial version of this sermon.

[4]Damian Thompson, *The End of Time: Faith and Fear in the Shadow of the Millennium* (Hanover, N.H.: University Press of New England, 1996), 226.

[5]*Lexington* (Ky.) *Herald-Leader*, 28 November 1998, C3.

Chapter 7: Revelation 5

[1]E.g., 1 Thessalonians was written because these Christians did not know how to understand deaths within their congregation. They had believed that the second coming would occur before anyone in their church died.

[2]This image also reminds one of Paul's understanding of ministry and of the Christian life as a life of strength in weakness.

[3]M. Eugene Boring, *Revelation*, Interpretation (Louisville, Ky.: John Knox Press, 1989), 112.

[4]I thank Nancy Turner, assistant professor of worship and music at Lexington Theological Seminary, for this perspective.

Chapter 8: Revelation 14

[1]For a good brief examination of Revelation that uses this outline, see Bruce Metzger, *Breaking the Code: Understanding the Book of Revelation* (Nashville: Abingdon Press, 1993).

[2]While the NRSV translates this verse by inserting "the" between "like" and "son of man," the definite article is not present in the Greek text. It is perhaps easier to understand who this figure is if we do not add the definite article, an article that makes the passage sound more like this personage in Jesus than the text actually warrants.

[3]James Melvin Washington, ed., *A Testament of Hope: The Essential Writings of Martin Luther King, Jr.* (San Francisco: Harper and Row Publishers, 1986), 286.

[4]Isa. 63:1–6; Lam. 1:15.

[5]"Persecution Plagues Christians," *Lexington* (Ky.) *Herald-Leader*, 31 October 1998, C7.

[6]Ibid.

[7]John Stackhouse, "India's Christians demand end to persecution," *The Globe and Mail* (Toronto, Ontario), 5 December 1998, A19.

[8]www.mcjonline.com/news/news2604.htm (14 December 1998).